HANDLE
WITH
CARE

A personal and
professional memoir

RACHAEL HEARSON

MIRROR BOOKS

First published by Mirror Books in 2020

Mirror Books is part of Reach plc
10 Lower Thames Street
London EC3R 6EN

www.mirrorbooks.co.uk

ISBN 978-1-913406-03-5

Typeset by Danny Lyle

Printed and bound in Great Britain by
CPI Group (UK) Ltd, Croydon, CR0 4YY

A CIP catalogue record for this book is available from the British Library.

Every effort has been made to fulfil requirements with regard to
reproducing copyright material. The author and publisher will be
glad to rectify any omissions at the earliest opportunity.

3 5 7 9 10 8 6 4 2

Cover images: Alamy and Trevillion

Dedicated to all of the amazing mothers and their families that I have been privileged to visit, and who have shared their journeys with me. Thank you.

To all the conscientious and diligent Health Visitors, who quietly move mountains the length and breadth of the country each and every working day.

Also to my loved ones, especially J, BB and GG. I heart you and do it all for you.

Introduction

The work of a health visitor is behind closed doors – largely hidden, yet no less profound. We have privileged and unique access to all families with children under five, our office is your living room. It is our remit to visit you at home. We are the only health professionals to do this when you have young children. It used to be that the family GP would do a 'courtesy' visit after the birth of a baby, but this no longer happens.

Our relationships with our clients are highly personal; we often see families at their most vulnerable. We deal in the full human experience. We get to talk about and witness life in all its messy, fluctuating yet awesome majesty.

I joined the NHS as a student nurse four decades ago. 9 July 1979, to be precise. Since then I have worked as a nurse, a midwife and, for the last 30 years, as a health visitor. You would have to be living on another planet to be unaware of the never-ending shifts in policy, treatments, delivery of care, contracts, expectations and ongoing financial challenges within the NHS.

When I started there were no computers, mobiles or project managers; there were no algorithms, policies for lone workers, key performance indicators or policy-wonk terminology. There was the GP, complete with collar, tie and good humour, who visited your home at 3am when your child had otitis media (earache), the community midwife who called at your home daily for at least 10 days after you or your partner had given birth, and the cheery health visitor who visited weekly to weigh your lovely baby until you were both happy that you had ironed out any issues – be they feeding, emotional or anything else, really. The frequency of visits was determined by how much reassurance you felt you needed or, conversely, by how quickly you got fed up with her input. Both judgements were equally valid as long as mum, baby and family were well. Sounds simple.

However, the reality is that I have been chased down an isolated stairwell by crack-addled, drug-addicted pimps and threatened by a knife-wielding wife beater in a homeless hostel. Unwittingly, I have visited a brothel, witnessing the usual activities upon, ahem, 'entering' the property. I've negotiated corrugated iron sheets to access the inner-city squat which a young family called home. The floor was bare concrete covered with a light coating of border collie fur. There was a mattress. A few strategically placed candles. No electricity or running water. And a 10-day-old baby.

I also had the opportunity of hoofing it to the daughter of a lady-in-waiting with her new baby. Their home was a famous historical house with royal connections and I was shown the room where Anne Boleyn slept prior to parting with her head.

We take all sorts of absurd and surreal scenarios in our stride. Inner-city London provided many a challenge. Indeed, I have had the, er, privilege of witnessing a 20-something male masturbating on a sofa while I discussed with his girlfriend the sex offenders' course they were both undertaking. Her boyfriend was an offender. His girlfriend was doing the partners' course.

The Young Chap jogged down the stairs and plonked himself on the sofa. I continued the conversation with his girlfriend, and there was a new baby to examine. Noticing some movement out of the corner of my eye, I glanced to my right, expecting him to be scratching an itch or fiddling with something. He was, in fact, doing both. There it was, the unmistakeable rhythmic wrist action, sustained and unrelenting. He was looking into the middle distance. Dear Lord. I shifted in my seat, with my back to him. If I can't see it, it's not happening. Then panic. Oh, Christ – what happens at 'lift off'...? At least there was an absence of sound effects. Every cloud. He left the room shortly after. His girlfriend, puzzlingly, did not acknowledge the situation. He carried on as though we weren't there; she carried on as though he wasn't there; I kept calm and just... carried on. Not the first or last time I'll be in the company of a wanker.

Investigating a toddler who appeared to have been left alone in a house in Tower Hamlets, a student nurse and I let ourselves in, as the back door was ajar and said child could have escaped. We eventually discovered the adult male who was allegedly in charge; he was drunk, in bed and snoring loudly, totally impervious to our shouting and bellowing for him to wake up. Police had to be called on that occasion as we couldn't leave the child in an unlocked house with an inebriated 'carer'.

I once visited a new baby and his young mother in a tattoo parlour – we were jammed next to several tanks of snakes and tarantulas. I found myself mesmerised by the clients awaiting their inkings, one of whom was sporting a pair of jeans covered in graffiti written in biro. 'Josh fucks goats.' 'Ellie-Mae takes it up the chuff.' It was all very compelling. When I asked Mum of New Baby about her name choices, she informed me that this particular babe was to be called Aimee-Porcha (sic).

I asked, 'As in Portia, the Shakespearean character?'

'No,' came the reply. 'As in the car.'

We make charity applications for washing machines or other white goods when you have run out of hope, cash, antidepressants, when there are 16 stained baby grows and the entire family's soiled undies to deal with and your Disability Living Allowance (DLA) has just been declined. We don't make a habit of it, but we might offer our own money if someone is in dire need. Maybe the cupboards are bare and it's Christmas. They might show you an empty purse. Or the bailiffs are threatening. You'd have to be a hard bastard to walk away.

I did a straw poll in the office recently, asking my lovely colleagues if they had helped any of their clients. There was a stiffening of spines as they stopped the tip-tapping on their keyboards and slowly turned around to share stories of having purchased groceries (pre-food banks) or maybe a food voucher for a family at Christmas. Very rarely will cash be given – it shouldn't be – but, in reality, it happens. Often, we are the only ones who get to witness the daily struggle for ordinary, hard-working families.

Food banks came into being pretty much at the time of the global collapse of the financial markets. Prior to 2004, the Trussell Trust, an anti-poverty charity that started in Salisbury, ran two food banks. In 2020 there is now a network of over

2,000; the Trussell Trust runs 1,200 of these, and the rest are organised by independent providers or charities.

Vouchers can be given out by social workers, GPs, health visitors and Citizen's Advice Bureau workers. Their standard provision at each referral is three days' worth of food for each family – typically tinned and dried goods which can be stored easily, although they are more likely to include some perishable goods since 2018, when food banks hooked up with Asda and similar. There are some packages that cater for those who have no access to proper cooking facilities and contain only food that can be heated in a microwave.

Between 2018 and 2019, the Trussell Trust gave out 1,583,668 parcels, which was up 18.8 percent on the previous year. If we include independent food banks, probably over 3 million parcels were distributed. The recipients of these parcels were likely to be experiencing problems with claiming benefits, divorce, unemployment, eviction, mental health, debt or any combination of these.

Our reality is that whilst we work amongst the most loving, insightful and functioning families, we have to focus our time, energies and thought processes on those that are the polar opposite. Those that are fractured and sometimes abusive to their children – either by acts of negligence (omission), for instance, leaving the children alone to go out drinking, or by wilful acts of harm (commission), from the smack, the cigarette burn or any other variation of physical, emotional or sexual abuse – and all points in between. Parents can sometimes be avoidant, evasive, hostile, threatening to us and possibly duplicitous – especially when under the spell of a partner just out of prison, a violent offender, a paedophile, a drug dealer/ user, someone with severe mental health problems, or any combination of these.

And yet health visiting is one of those professions that most people think is a bit of a non-job. 'You just sit on sofas and drink tea, don't you?' 'It's not like you're a real nurse, in the hospital.' 'My health visitor was bloody useless,' some will cry – more than is seemly. Well, we are real nurses. When I qualified, the State Registered Nurse (SRN) training lasted three years, then there would be a period of being a staff nurse or ward sister, followed by either a 12-week obstetric course or 12 to 18 months' training to be a midwife. After that you could begin your health visitor training.

More recently, health visitors train to degree level, as registered nurses, which takes three years, and then continue with the one-year health visiting course. A significant rump of us have studied at master's level. Unlike our amazing colleagues who continue to take the strain in the hospital fraternity, we are out there on our own. Whilst we carry a mobile, there is no immediate back-up team to call for help if we're stuck in a dicey situation. No tea breaks spent chatting in the canteen, nobody else to ask, 'Is this OK, what do you think?' On. Our. Own.

I sat in a B&B recently, in the communal dining room, with a young family. Greasy tables, cheap cutlery. Nasty placemats featuring the ubiquitous still-life fruit were laid out optimistically, as though awaiting some kind of Universal Credit banquet. A tatty pink tinselly Christmas tree stood forlornly on a side table. We chatted and the young man, owner of a pock-marked face and beer breath, told me that they had moved from York to this seaside town to escape nosy social care, who were chasing them as his girlfriend had had a sexual relationship with her father.

They had a two-year-old girl, who scowled at me and flapped her hands. She had no discernible speech and threw a cracked mobile phone at her mother. Bingo. A direct hit to the sternum. I spoke to them about referring their daughter for a speech and language assessment plus audiology, but they were gone again after a week. Headed to who knows where with no family or support. The flotsam and jetsam of the underclass in the UK today.

The level of real deprivation out here is staggering when you are up close and witness it each and every day.

For many of our clients, it's not just the lack of a place to call home, with all its attendant comforts, safety and privacy. It's the lack of dignity that this life of inadequate resources and instability confers on families. The absence of choice and self-determination is heartbreaking – imagine you and your family having to share and jostle for space with several strangers, using the same kitchen, loo, bathroom.

Clients in these situations may only just have clapped eyes on me and yet I am asking (hopefully sensitively) if they might explain their financial situation in order that I can advise, offer a food bank referral or 'sign post' – as is the new phrase – to some other resource that may help. They may not be claiming the full complement of financial aid. I may help with a request to a charity for a particular item or a timely, hard-hitting email to the local MP, or I could offer to write a letter to the relevant housing department or association advocating that they are expedited up the waiting list (a letter would historically have helped significantly, less so now due to hideously limited housing stock).

Most days I, like the majority of my colleagues, am outraged at the deprivation that families are forced to endure, and subsequently spend significant time on the blower, aggravating the relevant professional to try to get stuff done. Due to data privacy laws, we often have to do this while sitting with our clients so that they can give their permission for the agency to speak to us, on the client's behalf.

Hopefully, we have the warmth and compassion of Oprah, handy with the tissues when all your children have raging diarrhoea and you've just had unprotected sexual intercourse (UPSI) with your unreliable boyfriend – yes, I can bypass the dragon of a receptionist for that emergency contraception. We are often vociferous, barn-storming political activists when we need to 'get stuff done'. We are a nightmare for our NHS managers, as we are a rebellious bunch. Sure, we don't look so special when we are sitting on your sofa; we might look a bit staid, as though we've never had a real experience in our lives, but believe me, we have secured more refuge places for those fleeing violence (and helped them pack their bags) and seen more drug-addicted parents with their newborns than you can shake a stick at.

* * *

These are my professional and personal memoirs encompassing 40 years spent working in the NHS, as a nurse, midwife, health visitor and community practice teacher. Having undertaken a master's in health policy, planning and financing in 1996, I believed my future lay in management – strategic organising and delivery of the service and managing the staff in the lower tiers of management. It was dry to the point of desiccating all grey matter into the confidential waste shredder. I longed just to reconnect with the soul and wit of the Great British public full-time, to sit on their sofas, discussing their stories with a welcome coffee in hand.

After six months I was back, full throttle, to the front line – and it is where I am still privileged to be today. These reflections reveal some of the heart-rending, challenging and the downright bizarre situations that I have encountered during my time in the NHS.

Chapter One
The Bucket

I was born in 1960 in Devon to a Romany travelling family on my dad's side. We lived for most of my childhood in Barnstaple, adjacent to a pub on the banks of the River Yeo, a tributary of the Taw. Comedian Al Murray, the 'Pub Landlord', boasts of being born behind a box of crisps and swaddled in a damp promotional beer towel. I was christened with a Watneys Party Seven – the red barrel rolled out in the skittle alley along with the KP nuts.

Dad, Ronnie Taylor, came from a family of Irish wheelwrights, hawkers and medicine men – as a child, he would hold the tell-tale skull aloft whilst promoting potions at the fair. He worked for the Watneys brewery, and the house came with his job. On my mum's side, the family were Yorkshire miners. My grandfather on that side was a Labour councillor as well as a miner. Mum, Mary, is a keen church-goer, who still sports her 1940s hairdo. She worked in 'service' for a doctor and his family in Sheffield in her early teens, then in the 1940s moved on to a Lancashire cotton mill. This was followed by a stint in a Morecombe Bay hotel kitchen, where she met Dad. It was true love, apparently, as a damp dish cloth whizzed through the air, connecting with his 'fizzog' due to Dad's relentless teasing. Generous and kind to a fault, and a huge fan of *Countdown*, Mum is still razor sharp.

Home, beside the River Yeo, would flood regularly according to the cycles of the moon – which was a tad inconvenient as it rendered the cellar and the yard (which housed the outside lavvy) unusable. My childhood lavvy was not just any outside lavatory – sultry *M&S* tones here – but one *sans* electricity and packed to the gunnels with assorted arachnids, dangling from the ceiling and squatting in all corners, ready to strike. I would pee, peel off the medicated Izal (awful stuff – it used to spread everything rather than wipe), fix my gaze on the ceiling, finish with a 180-degree scan in case one of the eight-legged lodgers had decided to bungee jump down to my level, flush and run like hell.

A bucket, situated top left on the landing, was used when we couldn't access the lavvy. If you lingered too long, it left a red circular imprint on your arse. Our sewage system and associated hygiene were akin to a Dickensian slum.

I could never invite friends over, due to the lack of proper facilities, and developed a sense of otherness which has been hard to shift. If they called on me, my focus was always on the rapid wrapping up of their visit, instead of the usual long teenage mooning-about sessions, sharing David Cassidy posters, *Jackie* magazine and the inevitable angst. I got to be an expert at anti-hosting: withholding the offer of drinks and opening windows to create the required ambience to literally freeze them out. I ensured that they always had their coat on in preparation for a speedy departure. In predicting the length of time it took to fill a bladder, I could avoid at all costs the heart-sink request of, 'Where's the loo?'

The river that often cut us off from our outdoor lavvy ran smack bang through the middle of the town and was pivotal to the workings of manufacture and employment, certainly in the earlier part of the 20th century. Even during the 60s and 70s, there was a timber merchants' on the other side of the pub and a grain store on the other side of us. There was always lots of exciting activity to be seen by the river. Barges would dock with their cargoes of sand, which were then offloaded onto a tipper truck with a mechanical scoop and delivered to various builders' yards to be used in construction. There was always a presence of working men, cranes, boats, lorries – even a small train line to ferry the sand around to the other businesses in the vicinity.

More families lived on the other side of the grain store. One resident family had their own barge. Very occasionally I was invited out on a jolly river trip with all the other riverside dwellers. It was hugely exciting to jump aboard the noisy, diesel-engined vessel for a rare chug up the Yeo into the Taw and beyond, sea spray on our faces and freezing cold in thin anoraks. There was a real community spirit in our neighbourhood, despite the adversity.

One Sunday, out of the blue, a new barge rocked up and anchored just in front of our house. A new family – their boat was their home. Sailing around the country, mooring as they went, their children attended our school for about a month. We would sometimes walk there together, but no sooner had they anchored than they were off again. It was an unorthodox childhood. For them, for sure, but also for those of us resident by the quay.

We were all in this together. Everyone helped everyone else. The pub landlord would offer to cook a Sunday roast for us when Mum's cooker went kaput and, in true reciprocal fashion, his Sunday joint would arrive on our doorstep when he and his family had a power cut.

On one memorable summer, as a young teenager, I returned in the early evening to find the whole quay awash with water lapping at the front steps, due to a big spring tide. What a commotion! Everyone was out on their doorsteps, unable to go anywhere. I was stuck at the foot of the town bridge in sandals and bare legs, squealing at the prospect of having to wade across the flood to get home. Luckily a welly-toting neighbour came to the rescue. I was carried across the overflowing river and deposited onto the top step of our house without my toes ever touching the water.

The next-door Rolle Quay Inn was a source of entertainment, as folk would emerge swaying and clearly unfit to drive their car, parked immediately in front of the quayside. One such fella approached his vehicle unsteadily, managed to insert his key after several wildly inaccurate attempts, and promptly drove forward over the edge of the quay. The back end remained anchored on land and the front end dangled precariously over the edge with him in the driver's seat, tipped up in close proximity to the windscreen, scarily facing the river bed. There was much mirth and astonishment as drunk bloke and car had to be towed out. A wall was built pretty quickly after that to prevent similar mishaps.

Our bath was situated in the cellar, along with a mangle for wringing out the laundry – there was no washing machine, and Mum had to deal with bedsheets and other laundry in the bath by hand. Washing down there wasn't exactly the relaxing spa experience, either. There were also towering crates of beer, courtesy of Dad's monthly allowance. All the Watneys employees would get an allowance of beer and soft drinks in addition to their salary. When there was a high tide and an ensuing 12 inches of the River Yeo in the cellar, the crates would float loose from their stacking in the deluge, bobbing and clanking into each other, sounding for all the world like the clashing contraband in Falkner's *Moonfleet*.

There was a creaking, forbidding attic – no electricity again – that housed, amongst other things, huge great tea chests with assorted contents and a wind-up gramophone in its black case, with a heavy silver arm and stylus, on which I would play our several Mario Lanza LPs. Opera was, weirdly, one of the first genres of music I encountered.

One of my earliest memories is from my very first home, next to a 'chippy', where we lived briefly prior to the Watneys tied house. I remember watching my mother, hair in steel rollers, magnificent in her billowing nylon nightdress, performing the morning ritual of swooshing open the curtains for the Big Reveal: a mass of 'live' wallpaper – legions of writhing and scattering cockroaches. She would swish at them with a dustpan and brush, cursing vigorously and stamping on any escaping critter. The dead carapaces were wrapped in newspaper to sizzle on the coal fire.

I was astonished and appalled in equal measure by both her quiet determination and the horror of this experience to be repeated each day. My mother and I have never talked about this or anything else from the past. For her, the past is off-limits, and resolutely so. To be fair, she should be chuffed with how she coped with it all.

We shared our next home, the brewery one, with an inordinate number of mice, rats and spiders; if it had four, six or eight legs, it was likely to be resident. There was also a lot of freezing cold lino and green paintwork. There were lots of scamperings and scratchings at night. When Dad went out for a drink on a Saturday night, which he often did, Mum and I would watch Roald Dahl's *Tales of the Unexpected*, frighten ourselves witless, go up to bed, listen for the scratching and pitter-patter of tiny rodent feet and get even more scared until we heard the key go into the lock, which indicated Dad's return. Aaah. Breathe easy again. It's just mice, I would say to myself then. What was I scared of? No problem at all.

When a resident rat pegged it under the floorboards, there was a distinctive smell that was never forgotten. Dad would isolate the relevant plank, hoick out the offending creature and pop it in a carrier bag; I would be instructed to run down to the river and throw it into the estuary when no one was looking, before walking away nonchalantly, whistling, with hands in pockets.

I knew my dad's dad as Granfer. I'm not sure how long he was with us. He was permanently wedged behind the kitchen door with his gammy leg elevated on a chair, flat cap over one eye, crunching butterscotch. He had been a Traveller, selling fish from a horse and cart. The horse one day took exception to something or other and kicked him quite comprehensively; the ensuing ulcer never healed.

My dad was one of 11 children and a first-generation settler. I believe that nine survived. Having lived an itinerant lifestyle, his family – who were Travellers, or Gypsies as they were called at that time – attempted to settle down, selling fish and riveting china for the landed gentry, but still speaking Romany. (By the way, 'chav' is most definitely a Romany word, as in 'Mung, chavvy, mung'. Roughly translated, this means, 'Look sad and snivel, child, in order that the nice person will feel sorry for you and give you some money.')

Non-Gypsies were *gorjers*. And the whole point of the Romany language is that it is impenetrable to the *gorjers*. Once it becomes commonplace and understood, it's rendered useless and entirely new words have to be dreamt up to out-fox and deceive the everyday non-woodland folk. Some words are interchangeable with cockney rhyming slang. 'Mince pies', as in eyes. Del Boy's 'cushti', as in good.

Romany is also inextricably linked with Polari, a secret language which was used in fairgrounds, theatres, circuses, by Punch and Judy showmen and at sea. It is a mixture of rhyming slang, backslang, sailor slang and thieves' cant.

Words that come from Polari include: bevvy – drink; strides – trousers; kip – lodgings. David Bowie's 2016 album *Blackstar* contained a song, 'Girl Loves Me', which was largely in Polari. It was also used in the gay community in the 1960s.

My paternal grandmother, who I never met, was also a Gypsy, selling flowers, herbs, pegs and telling fortunes. I gather that she had excellent people-reading skills and worked out what they wanted to hear. Though who am I to be cynical? Perhaps she did indeed know a thing or two. Her surname was 'Wheelwright' and I understand she originated from Wexford, Ireland.

After leaving Devon as a young man, my father joined the Navy and fought in the Second World War. He sailed across to the USA in 1941 aged 20 to pick up a Brooklyn Yard minesweeper. From there he sailed to South America. His appendix was whipped out in West Africa and he was all but drowned off the coast of Norway – his ship was bombed and consequently sank in the North Sea off Narvik. News reached his family that he was lost, presumed dead.

However, he was picked up and returned to the bosom of his family. In keeping with a great many servicemen and women, his near drowning and wartime experiences were never really discussed thereafter. But I know it was irritating for him that, even after fighting for his country, his parents refused to entrust him with his own key to their rented house.

Post-war, after a spell as a bookies' 'runner' (which was illegal) and debt collector, he began working for the brewery, progressing from drayman to a fitter of beer taps, pipes and coolers for the array of Watneys pubs in the North Devon area. For this, he drove a British Leyland Comma van and I would sit in the middle on the engine as a child when we tootled around town – no seatbelts, of course.

His next vehicle was a red Hillman Avenger estate. He loved his job and enjoyed very much – too much really – the perks that accompanied his work, often regaling us with tales of having a 'half' in each pub that he visited 'just to be sociable'. It's quite horrifying, I know, but it's how it was. This was pre-drink-driving laws and breathalysers. I'm not sure how he avoided accidents, if I'm honest, but avoid them he did.

It was also his job to carry Granfer up the winding staircase to bed every night. He clearly struggled. His face would contort, turning purple; the sinews in his neck popping out like violin strings under the strain. I remember clearly Dad's fat belly protruding out from between a dinner-stained vest and trousers, braces dangling down his backside. How uncomplaining he was with roles reversed, carrying his father in his arms like a child.

When Dad was little, Granfer would take off to St Thomas' Hospital in London when the gammy leg was playing up. This was an event heralded by all nine children being dropped off to the workhouse for safe keeping until his return, where their heads were usually shaved due to nits.

Food was gruel based, the drink of the day was tea but, astonishingly, meat would feature on the menu, if only occasionally. Generally, though, it was all about creating conditions so bloody awful no one would ever want to return. There were tales of being on bread and water if someone had been quarrelling or fighting, and if caught slacking there was no cheese for a week. Residents were even sent before the magistrate and imprisoned if there was a combination of swearing, insurrection and refusal to work. It was something of which Dad was understandably ashamed and I intuited that I shouldn't raise the subject.

When I was around 10, we started to go 'Oop North' for holidays. It was a bit of a trek. Suitcases in hand, Mum and I would catch a series of trains to Sheffield, another to Doncaster, then a bus to her home village of Thurnscoe. We would stay with Mum's parents, Nan-nan and Granddad. There was the ubiquitous heap of coal in the street outside their council house – Granddad was a miner at Hickleton Main and this was part of the remuneration package from the National Coal Board.

Most houses had their coal outside in the street, delivered by tipper truck and left in a heap. A German shepherd, Rajah, and border collie, Shep, met us enthusiastically at the back gate, which served as the house's main entrance. Nan-nan would get in special things for us to enjoy on our visit. Lurpak (I know, I hadn't lived), orange juice in a milk bottle, Yorkshire curd tart. We would fetch sherry in a jug or other vessel by the quart for Granddad from the cask in the grocer's shop on the 'top road'. He seemed to survive on only liver, onions, garlic and sherry and went on well into his nineties. When he eventually became ill, everyone was panicking as they couldn't find his GP. Not registered anywhere. He must have one, surely? Transpires he didn't. Hadn't seen a doctor in decades.

Women wore their hair in the obligatory scarf and curlers all week, only to unleash it on a Saturday night when everyone would schlep up to the club, again 'on't top road'. Warm Watneys was served liberally; jukeboxes – all the rage in that era – belted out 'Love Grows' by Edison Lighthouse at ear splitting decibels. Most had a fag on the go dangling from the lower lip, smoke curling into one eye and still, though hopelessly sloshed, could yap and natter all night with lots of cries of, 'Ta-ra, Chuck', before wobbling and wending their way home.

I was included in the Saturday night trips up to the club and felt very grown up. I loved the sense of excitement and anticipation of getting ready, putting on our best togs. Mum worked in Fosters menswear and could get a discount on their unisex clothes, so I wore Falmer jeans, a denim jacket and a selection of cheesecloth shirts – I think it was fashionable in the mid-70s to wear men's clothes. Or perhaps it was just me? I was also in possession of a purple suede skirt with a matching purple knitted top that tied at the neckline in a criss-cross fashion. I adored the ensemble and thought I was the bee's knees. Accompanied by a red pair of platform lace-up shoes, of course. Purple and red. What a sight!

We would be driven by Uncle John to Great Aunt Mary's at Holme-On-Spalding-Moor near Market Weighton in the East Riding of Yorkshire. The visit would send me into raptures. She and her husband, Jack, lived on a farm. I'd love to tell you all about the bucolic lifestyle but I didn't get caught up in that. Bugger the farm – Great Aunt Mary could cook! She laid on homemade offerings of gargantuan proportions for our visit – nothing shop-bought here. The farmhouse table would groan with scones, jams, Yorkshire curd tart, Victoria sponge, home roasted hams, chutneys, brawn, great slabs of butter, a huge split tin loaf, pork pies, salads – which were just butterhead lettuce leaves and tomatoes back then, no dressing – nowt fancy, maybe a drizzle of vinegar – just perfectly plain farmhouse fayre. Oh Lord, it was a veritable feast and a highlight of the trip for me.

As we ate, there was family chatter and gossip, with disapproving and hushed tones used for certain relatives. I loved listening to the prevailing wisdom of the day being de-bunked: 'This "margarine is best for you" malarkey, what's that all about? Your great-grandmother, she lived till she was a hundred and all she ate were butter, cream and full fat milk – worra lowd o' nonsense.'

The north-facing larder fascinated me. The comforting smell of order and preparedness and knowing you were not going to run out of comestibles. There was always something in. There was only one drawback of a visit to the farm – lavatory related, of course. Whenever I asked to go for a wee, there were always uncomfortable exchanges of looks and it was suggested I go for a tiddle outside, somewhere, anywhere, really. Mum would walk me to the back door and holding onto my shoulders, would point me in the direction of a shed and whisper, 'Behind there'. Where does everyone else go? I mused. Perhaps it's a bucket situation again, I laughed to myself. What is it with my family and the deficit in the lavvy department?

Trilby-toting Jeremy Thorpe played a huge part in helping families escape sub-standard dwellings to be allocated somewhere homelier at this time. He was God-like to us in North Devon during the 1960s and 70s. We refused to believe the Norman Scott thing. After all, Thorpe appeared to genuinely care about injustice, and worked tirelessly doing good deeds.

I accompanied my Mother to several political election rallies as a child which were intoxicating to me. On dark nights after supper, Mum and I would take the short walk to Barnstaple cattle market in the rain for the rousing and theatrical speeches, the humour, the packed crowds cheering and the applause. On the stump, the lights illuminating the various prospective and hopeful candidates, it was magnificent – I loved it all and learnt to appreciate the power of politics and persuasion, right there.

I'm not sure if an MP helped Mum and Dad escape the bucket and floods by assisting with the allocation of their one-bed flat after I left home. North Devon was Liberal for decades but by the 1980s, it had gone Tory.

Apart from a burgeoning interest in politics, my other love was pop music. My sister, who is 10 years older than me, gave me – her annoying little sister – a transistor radio, as she had upgraded. It had a brown leather case and an earpiece so that I could listen to Radio Caroline under the bedclothes at night.

I kept a pen and paper under the bed to make a note of the music that I wanted to buy when I could purchase a much-desired stereo system. One of my first LP purchases when I eventually got my stereo was a disappointing compilation

Top of the Pops album – I didn't realise that the songs weren't performed by the original musicians. My very kind Uncle John had bought me the stereo in 'Donny' (Doncaster) when we were on our 'up north rail-and-road trip'.

Noel Edmonds was on air on Radio 1 each morning to accompany brekky. On the walk to school, we would break into song as we dawdled, gradually accruing our gang at various junctures. The sweet shop was the first pit stop, to purchase staple pineapple chunks for break time later. The tuck shop at school was always an option, too. We would eat a grapefruit before scoffing a Marathon (now a Snickers), absolutely, totally, certain that the former would cancel out the calories of the latter.

We benefitted from a purpose-built sixth-form centre where we could bring our records to play during break – there was a proper booth with turntable plus a microphone to do the DJing. We played music for ourselves, of course, and were responsible for inflicting some obscure and esoteric stuff on the others, too. Of course, there were always requests for ABBA, who were big at the time.

I was always considered bright at school, but a crisis of confidence occurred at the time of O levels. All my friends were going on the French exchange trip and I wasn't. After all, no one could be expected to do a return trip to ours – '*Fabrice, voulez-vous utiliser le Bucket?*' It was the first time that

I'd felt publicly isolated. I couldn't go and felt a tiny bit of me give up. Well, quite a bit, actually. There was so much excitement surrounding the whole experience regarding the returning French students – their accents, what they ate, what they refused to eat.

My peers and their families took Claudette or Emmanuel out to local hostelries; lots of families assembled in restaurants or places of interest so that the French students could socialise with their friends. The whole of the school seemed to come together as a community, a family even, energised in a collective effort to ensure that the French exchange pupils felt welcome, included and had fun. It seemed like a huge bonding experience for those who shared in all the thrilling activities my friends appeared to grow from it too, especially after their own experiences with *their* families in Calais. Somehow, they exuded more confidence, not only in terms of their French expertise but in *every* way, it seemed.

I was excluded from the whole thing and, annoyingly, French was one of my best subjects. My confidence withered, my future and how I viewed it shrank and it stung, badly.

I learned that I had done badly in my exams whilst working in an Anadin factory for the summer. The machines hummed and whirred; conveyor belts shunted endlessly and noisily – shades of *Made in Dagenham*. Donna Summer played incessantly throughout an idyllic summer of 1977 – not quite as hot as '76, but almost. We were sent home at one point, as the factory had overheated.

I was on the reject Anadins. We had to repackage them and place them into a drum thing. The supervisor would approach us periodically to tell us off if we had been chatting too much and hadn't achieved the targeted number. That same supervisor would wheel her trolley around the factory each Friday afternoon when the air buzzed with the anticipation of a weekend revelling. She dispensed the small brown envelopes with a clear window revealing your name and £25 in cash for the week's endeavour. We skylarked, joked and flirted our way through that glorious summer, though the experience was marred toward the end by my terrible exam results. I had only gained three O levels! English Language, English Literature and French. I cried for a week and then decided that it was not going to define me.

I signed up to do A level French, as it was the subject that was likely to have a limited shelf life unless I continued with it, and repeated a few 'O's that September – the plan was to then continue full-time with A levels. I really wanted to study English language and literature at university, though without really knowing what I would do with it thereafter. Oh well. I re-sat the Os successfully – hurrah! – but despite the dream of uni life, I knew that no one in my family had 'gone before', as they say, and so I didn't know if it was possible financially. I intuited it wasn't.

So, I did a stint of voluntary work at the Alexandra Hospital, a former workhouse in Barnstaple (the very same that my dad had been deposited in as a child) and got a weekend job at a nursing home, to see if I was suited to nursing. I concluded that I was, and I decided to ditch the A levels and apply to train as a nurse. In the absence of doing what I truly wanted to do (English at university, at that time) then at least, I thought, I could be useful. I think it was about compromise at that point.

Nursing felt right: it was a course that would provide structure and an end goal. And, hurrah, I would earn a salary. More importantly, I could see that nursing was the perfect fit for me. I had the right amount of inclination and aptitude and some degree of intellectual spark that refused to be dampened. I *can* do this, I told myself. It was a pragmatic decision, and was helped by the fact that nursing came with a side order of respectability for the likes of me, who came from family who hadn't really had any kind of profession at all, with the exception of Dad, who had become a blue-collar semi-skilled worker.

I worked briefly as a receptionist at a GP's surgery for a few weeks prior to starting nurse training. The girls were sweet, supportive and reassuring in their matching waistcoats and skirts. I had an early introduction to the doctors' illegible handwriting, snippets of Latin and the tedious task of filing results into the small cardboard pouches that historically stored health records – all notes, results, referrals, communications – everything is computerised now.

I grew up to be a bit shy. It's such an unforgiveable, distasteful quality, isn't it? Except, for a lot of us, when we have something concrete to say, something we truly believe in – heart, soul, cells, molecules, the whole shebang – we are paradoxically not shy at all.

It was definitely easier for working-class folk like me in the 70s, what with being paid to train as a nurse – that quaint, old-fashioned concept of remuneration. We were paid a monthly salary of around £200 basic and extra for night duty and weekends. Some months we were flush with over £300. Our rent for our room in the nurses' home was deducted from our salary, so our net pay was ours to spend or save.

It was harder for some nurses to make ends meet if they lived out of nurses' accommodation, as they had rent and bills to pay, and certainly with the advent of tuition fees and maintenance loans and the scrapping of bursaries it became much worse. Most student nurses now get by with the help of parents or a generous partner, as it's close to impossible if you are completely reliant on your loan. In recent years, I have encountered some who eat only occasionally. Like it's optional. Shall I dine off organic ozone today?

Not long ago, one student nurse came to spend some time with me for her community module, which is a short period of a few weeks during the paediatric nurse training where student nurses join us out in the community, rather than just in a hospital base. She looked a shade of greenish grey that could be included in a posh paint colour palette under the soubriquet 'starving nurse'. Heck, I could do a whole new colour range for them. What about 'politician's cheek' for starters? I asked when she had last eaten.

'Ah, I'm fine. Really. I ate yesterday morning.'

It was 2pm the following day. That's great then. Thank you to all the decision-makers who got their education for free. We know who you are. It's interesting to know that in all the countries of Europe, higher education costs a fraction of ours of what it costs to students here; we are the only European country to indebt our young people to such eye-watering sums.

Anyhow, it was my privilege to take her to anywhere she wanted for lunch. She opted for a Macky D's and wolfed a double thingummy-burger with fries – she went large. It truly was a Happy Meal. Until the next day, presumably, when it was back to packet noodles, 35p Lidl, the new poor person's filler-upper. I gather that the present government is reinstating the bursary.

They need to make good on that promise.

Chapter Two
Bart's Tarts

On 9 July 1979, I left home as Mum and Dad cried on the front step, to train as a state registered nurse (SRN) at St Bartholomew's – Bart's, as everyone calls it – a London teaching hospital.

Rahere, a monk and court jester to Henry I, built the hospital for the poor on the site of West Smithfield in 1123, following a dream. Hogarth painted the awe-inspiring canvasses, 'The Good Samaritan' and 'Pool of Bethesda', that adorn the impressive staircase to the oak-panelled great hall, also abundantly lined with the portraits of celebrated surgeons and medics, such as Percival Pott, James Paget, John Abernethy and William Harvey, all of whom have wards named after them. This is where the grandest of grand formal gatherings take place. The square, with its fountain, is the epicentre of the Gibbs design, and a celebrated architectural piece in itself.

I'd originally been down for training locally in Devon, but I'd really wanted to start my own life. So I sent off for the pamphlet outlining the training and requirements at Bart's, applied, and after a surprisingly successful interview with a slightly formidable Miss Gribble, I was permitted to join the hospital's hallowed corridors.

As the date for moving to London grew nearer, I felt increasingly apprehensive about the whole prospect. I felt intimidated and thought perhaps I was asking too much of myself, and I also wondered if I would find others there who were similar to me. Thankfully, I did, but the truth was that *everyone* was really welcoming and reassuring.

My boyfriend – who I had met on a blind date and looked a bit like Roger Hodgson from Supertramp – drove me up in his pale green Ford Cortina, wearing a Genesis T-shirt, jeans, plimsolls and his brown plastic car coat with fake fur collar, to the strains of *Tubular Bells*, Pink Floyd's *Wish You Were Here* and KC & The Sunshine Band playing from a knackered cassette.

As instructed, all my worldly possessions were in two cardboard boxes: flared jeans, rugby shirt, cowboy boots, two tie-dye dresses, a Laura Ashley royal blue floral maxi dress, undies, a kettle and some nondescript floral bedding from Timothy Whites, plus a purse, a Lloyds cheque book and a bank card. That was it. Feeling sick with anxiety and eager anticipation, I began my professional journey as a first-year 'grey belt', which would expose me to a whole new world of independence and give me professional skills. A feminist energy crackled in this new era of Margaret Thatcher as PM. Regardless of her politics, you knew she was different and a radical.

On arriving in our allocated rooms, we were greeted by a letter from the previous occupant who could move on when a new intake arrived. It outlined the time and room number of where the tea and cakes were being served to welcome the new cohort. So every year, with the arrival of every new 'set', the newbies would be welcomed into the fold by the older girls, thereby fostering inclusivity and nurturing; there was to be no skulking in our bedrooms, alone. Socialise, chat and get to know each other were the instructions – nay, orders of the day. You were a worry if you weren't seen mixing it up and joining in.

Lucy Butter was the previous incumbent of room 636 and at 3pm on that Sunday, 9 July, I went along to her new room for the tea party. I knocked at the door and was invited in by a chummy, smiley gal to be introduced to a host of other newbies. I had found my tribe, and so my new life began.

I was measured up for my uniform the following day in a packed, whirring, industrious sewing room. Row upon row of ladies sat at sewing machines immersed in yards of material for uniforms. We felt valued. Important even. There were strict rules about uniform on duty and not wearing uniform outside unless you had your cape on in the immediate environs – for instance, walking around the adjacent streets – and donning your standard-issue gabardine mac when travelling on the tube.

We wore heavy cotton black and white pin-striped dresses with a card-like white collar attached with studs at the neck, over which a white starched linen apron was tied. Our heavy black capes had red cross-over straps across the bosoms that fixed at your waist at the back.

The hat was always a mystery to me. Even after three years, I never really mastered them. The finished article had shades of the historical headwear you associate with Florence. It was usually made on an upside-down saucepan or an item of a similar size and shape. A large rectangular piece of starched white linen was folded over several times to form a thick band which was then wrapped around the pan. It was pinned where the two sides came together. The flailing remains at the back would be tucked over and up in a large double-diamond-shaped tail. Most gals were neat and prim. 'Nurse Taylor, your hat looks like a crumpled sail.'

I was 18 years old and my new life had a structure and routine that felt manageable and rewarding. There was a balance between working on the wards, studying in the school of nursing and giddying around London. Overall, it was a safe, kind and most agreeable place to be. It was traditional and tranquil during the day, then at night many a rugby-playing medical student was chucked into the historic fountain, drunk and fully clothed, to a chorus of ribald rugby ditties.

There were scary sisters in their royal blues and tall white hats and more relatable senior staff nurses known as 'pinks', due to their pale denim dresses in the distinctive shade of blush. They floated effortlessly from emptying bedpans to administering intravenous injections. Consultants did their rounds in a haze of becalmed splendour and unflappable efficiency. Dear Lord, may I reach the pinnacle of being a 'pink' one day, was our ultimate prayer.

I was so unworldly on arrival, even though I had a boyfriend. It took me at least until the second year, moving from novice grey belt to second-year striped belt, to work out that a few of the girls were there to find a doctor for a husband. It hadn't occurred to some of us. I think I was a little naïve at the outset and totally shocked at the prospect that such a thing could be a possibility. I was there to be useful – as I had always wanted to be.

Most were so much more sophisticated than me. They seemed quite exotic and knowing, with phrases such as,

'I expect I'll see Roger this weekend; he's invited me to his cottage – just outside Bath.' Gosh, these girls actually know chaps of a similar age who own cottages! That was a whole new level of wealth and adulthood.

We were known colloquially as Bart's Tarts – something which was a claim to fame, a badge of honour, even if it wasn't entirely accurate. It implied a tribal belonging – most of us weren't tarty at all.

There was a certain type that formed a significant rump of the group. It seemed they had parents, siblings or relatives who were in the medical profession and had trained at Bart's too. Their Father might have been a consultant, or something in the City, or perhaps a journalist or the MD of a FTSE company. Some were in receipt of a very generous allowance from their parents and didn't have to worry about the salary as some of us did. You just knew they were different. They pronounced and strangulated vowels, and the unwavering confidence and private schooling gave them away. I wandered around, initially at least, with all my worldly goods in a crumpled plastic carrier, exuding the fragrance of fry-ups, coal-tar soap and Vosene, while they smelt of Rive Gauche, Marlboros and money.

I began to feel a certain unease on occasions. I don't think it was something that was identified at that point.

Imposter syndrome. I fleetingly questioned, 'Am I good enough to be here?' The self-doubt would appear periodically and settle in the pit of my stomach and mind, festering and churning like an unwanted spell. Expelliarmus!

I couldn't help but feel that my peers came with a side order of connection and gravitas that I just didn't have. I guess this was my opportunity to reinvent myself. And I was always going to make the best of my given circumstances, seeing as I had no alternative. As so many working-class girls and boys know, when there is no family money or back-up, you *have* to make it work. Besides, when I got to know them, even the posh girls were nice and sociable, and it was beyond fun.

My tribe were pretty similar and working class, too. We hung out, cooked, ate, drank, studied and partied together. We frequented Chas 'n' Dave's Chapel Market for cheap pots and pans, and I would flex my Access card for trips to Miss Selfridge and make small, stupid purchases from Harrods to prove I'd shopped there – a begonia from the plant hall (good grief, why?) or a Christmas pudding in December to take home. We'd also go to C&A and Bourne & Hollingsworth on Oxford Street. Their demise ushered in the era of Top Shop, Jane Norman and Wallis. Liberty was a favourite place to wander aimlessly around, imagining our grown-up selves wearing something elegant in *Strawberry Thief*, donning it carelessly with a pair of elegant Maud Frizon's and possibly an antique Cartier Tank, inherited from a distant relative. Oh, how we dreamed.

I discovered Tony Benn and punk. Not a cliché at all. I had a gradual political and professional awakening during my training, culminating in a full-blown epiphany whilst ensconced on the floor in Collets Bookshop, Charing Cross Road, where I discovered Ian Kennedy and his thought-provoking tome, *The Unmasking of Medicine*. He argued that medicine had taken a wrong path to scientific reductionism and that doctors' decisions were not always scientific or even medical, but often social and political. I questioned everything going forward. Still do, much to the annoyance of my managers.

After spending an inordinate amount of time in Collets, a famously left-wing outlet, and joining CND at a later date, I experienced a spate of receiving my mail already opened. It didn't last long. I was clearly not who or what they thought I was (whoever 'they' were). I didn't last long in CND either, not having been present at Greenham Common or attended the requisite local groups and gatherings. I was a lefty in thought but not so much in deed. I preferred another kind of party, to be fair. The jolly, drinking sort.

* * *

We spent the first six weeks at Bart's in the school of nursing, returning at various intervals thereafter, as we learned the ropes. We made beds, practised our injection techniques on oranges and resuscitation techniques on the plastic dummy, 'Resusci-Annie'. There was anatomy and physiology to get to grips with, essay-writing, practical assessments and, in our spare time, scooching around London, availing ourselves of the splendid free tickets allocated to London nurses for the theatre, Wimbledon fortnight, art exhibitions and more.

On occasion, we treated ourselves by dining out on wholefoods at Cranks; Garfunkel's was beginning to make an entrance as Bernie Steak Houses faded out. We drank copiously at the cocktail bars in Covent Garden – LS Grunts, Fatso's Pasta Joint – or feasted on nasi goreng and satay at the Rasa Sayang, Leicester Square. Heavenly. On a few occasions an anonymous diner bought myself and my boyfriend our desserts and a brandy to top the meal off. The waiter would explain that we 'looked so delighted with every mouthful' that it made the generous donor happy. Never discovered who they were. But how sweet was that? And all while still saving £50 per month on a student nurse's salary. 40 years ago. What happened?

It should be said that the state registered nurse (SRN) training was structured differently in the 70s to the registered nurse training of today. Back then, we got in with O and A levels – I clearly got in on Os – and we worked in a variety of settings in those three years. There were adult medical and surgical wards, initially, then usually 12-week placements in various other specialities: paediatrics, geriatrics, psychiatry, obstetrics, gynaecological wards, theatres, A&E, a bit of community work. (I spent some time with a health visitor in Hackney, which is what first piqued my interest.)

Then you returned to Bart's, usually as a third year, with more responsibility – you'd run wards on nights and take on more during the day with consultant ward rounds and, perhaps, sometimes be the most senior nurse on duty, ensuring that you could handle the required responsibility and decision-making. By spending an allotted time in differing settings, we could decide which speciality we wanted to go into.

Nowadays, the training is divided into adult, children's, mental health and learning disability nursing, so you have to work out what branch of nursing you want to specialise in before actually trying it which, for those of us who got to try various specialities as part of our training, doesn't quite make sense, but it's how it is.

My first female medical ward at Bart's dealt in harrowing malignant melanomas; it was also my first exposure to death. A shockingly young woman in her thirties – tall, educated and well spoken – was reduced to a bed-ridden existence, in a selection of pink floral nighties and suffering agonising pain, as I recall. There were regular, efficiently timed-to-the-minute injections of morphine, but it didn't seem to touch her and it all seemed highly unsatisfactory. You learn very quickly that both life and death can be very arbitrary and unworthy of such egregious injustice.

Here we were duly bossed around by a ward sister who, despite her tiny, pocket-sized frame, was fearless. Assertive to the point of authoritarian, she would take anyone on, including the scariest of consultants and us nurses if she felt we were slacking in the bedpan or hospital corner departments. For such a diminutive figure, she had a big personality with equivalent voice, but it was all entirely appropriate, even necessary, somehow. Nowadays, I would think there might be all sorts of allegations of 'bullying', but it all worked and we respected her.

My second ward was paediatric oncology, where all the children had some form of cancer. I felt unprepared, overwhelmed and useless. In the end, faced with my inability to fathom a disease of such magnitude, I reasoned that I should give way to the things I could fathom: establishing relationships with the patients, their parents and siblings and my colleagues, focusing on the familiar routine of the ward and its procedures.

My own need to develop and survive became under-pinned with the awareness that kindness really is everything. We could play with our patients (reading, jigsaws, Lego, painting) or fetch Coca-Cola and crisps when they fancied – all the usual childish prerequisites. We could attempt to alleviate their pain by way of regular analgesia and keeping spirits up. That much we could do. Ultimately, we avoided contemplating a universe in which tiny children with retinoblastomas – cancer of the eye (and an accompanying enucleation: removal of the eye) – were even a thing.

Some of my colleagues became the 'favourites' there; they could charm and joke with the senior ward sister who was revered and God-like to me, but I always held back – the shyness thing again – and watched as the others secured their places to return as staff nurses. Ah, so that how it goes, I thought, thinking that I would never secure a position. Still, it was only my second ward. There was plenty of time to find my feet.

Next stop was male surgical. Here I had my first foray into night duty, where I learnt that I would cry before each dreaded night shift and, puzzlingly, be absolutely fine once engaged in the discharging of my duties on the ward. Enthusiastic even. I gather that it is a common phenomenon. I would wake up at 3pm after a night shift and fret about what would happen if I couldn't do it, or who I was doing nights with.

I also had a severe propensity for inappropriate giggling on nights – hysteria more than likely, but there you are – and it was always important that when there were just two of us running a ward, I wouldn't be met with a stony, disapproving face when I found something ridiculous or absurd. It was good to be working with a like-minded soul who shared the humour. Usually, I went to the sluice to let it out, or sisters' side room. Of course, we didn't just run around laughing like loons (patients were asleep), but somehow it felt that the worry and responsibility and the 'what ifs?' were much more manageable if you laughed at things.

Once a colleague burnt her hat putting food in the ward cooker to heat. On other occasions there would be general merriment about donning a pair of animal feet slippers (stout lace-ups were the order of the day). If a nursing officer failed to look down and spot the ridiculous footwear, there would be much delight in having got away with it. There was the spraying of Op-site on the cockroaches as they appeared each night. This was a protective film to be sprayed on a wound post operatively, but we found it most useful for disabling the critters as it stopped them in their tracks. Then a braver one – usually me, being the expert – would scoop them up to put in the bin.

Snacks would be brought in and shared with the SHOs, the on-call doctors who would do a last ward round of the evening before attempting to sleep. We only called them in extremis, but if someone was admitted for an emergency operation, they would have to be beckoned and arrangements made for surgery or whatever the situation entailed.

We would do the last drug round of the day and dim the lights to encourage the patients to settle down. Some would keep their bedside overhead lamp on for reading. There were always fluid charts to add up, blood pressures and general obs to undertake, and some would need various pain relief or other medication throughout the night. There were always things to prep for the following day, maybe organising X rays and notes for a consultant's round the next day. Then we sometimes caught up with some revision from the medical books in the ward cupboard whilst sitting at the nurse's station if we had a quiet moment.

The first night of a run of night shifts was about pushing on through the challenges and tasks that arose on the ward, having been awake all day. I think because of that, the first night was the most overwhelming: at Bart's, the prospect of seven nights on (followed by six off) would be yawning ahead, while it was eight nights at St Leonard's, Shoreditch, with seven off. But once in the swing of things, and having found common territory with your colleague, there would be a natural momentum which propelled you, happily, forward.

* * *

I became a second-year nursing student, known as a 'striped belt'. My placements were at Hackney Hospital, The Mother's Hospital, and St Leonard's Hospital too.

I lived as well as worked in Hackney, as we had lodgings in one of the two hospital accommodation blocks. I saw it all there – from caring for the elderly to witnessing extreme psychotic behaviour on the psychiatric ward (F block), as well as the hysterectomies and terminations on the gynae wards, and much more besides.

St Leonard's, Shoreditch, was made famous by the heroic nurse Edith Cavell, who was shot for harbouring Allied soldiers in the First World War. I undertook my obstetric secondment at the Mothers' Hospital, Clapton, a Salvation-Army-run hospital (it was demolished some years later to make way for a housing development). At the time I duly rejected the notion of entering midwifery, after witnessing my first delivery under the melting heat of the satellite-dish-sized overhead spotlights, while rigged up in a green gown on top of my uniform and wearing a blue 'papery' hat. I cringed at the grisly crunch of scissors into intimate flesh by way of an episiotomy.

Later, though, I did a volte-face. I decided I rather liked the immensity, import and joy of delivering babies. Once you had acclimatised to the blood and heat and the potential drama, it was incredibly rewarding. Who wouldn't be happy at the prospect of delivering new life and the marvel of it all? (I didn't ever become acclimatised to the episiotomies, though. They were always undertaken with a heavy heart.)

Lank-haired Doris would wander out of Hackney Hospital's F block in her tartan coat and matching slippers whatever the weather, clutching her oversized handbag and, with a sweet smile, would ask passers-by for 10p for the bus to Stoke Newington. If the reply was in the negative, the girly smile would vanish into a snarl with an instruction to 'Fuck off, then!' Sometimes, if feeling particularly 'feisty', she would swing the handbag in the direction of said refusenik's kidney region.

Oxy-Jim, as he was known, was one of the legendary and much treasured porters. 'Gimme some more effing spuds,' was one of his favourite refrains, oft heard in the canteen queue. Jim was responsible for transporting highly flammable cylinders of oxygen (hence his name – combination of oxygen and James, you get my drift) around the hospital grounds, which he always did with a fag on the go, dangling from the bottom lip. Utterly incomprehensible nowadays with the rabid health and safety laws. He could have easily have vaporised into Explosi-Jim.

Various patients from F block went out and about during the day as they were there on a voluntary basis. One young man sporting a black suit and a Homburg would astonishingly stop the heaving traffic by walking into the road with a raised arm and hand – buses would screech to a halt and allow him to cross with much tooting of horns and Anglo-Saxon profanity.

At night (we lived next to the psychiatric wing) there was the frequent dinging of fire alarms as the residents of F block would set fire to their beds with an unextinguished fag, having fallen asleep. With sighs of, 'Oh Christ – not a-bloody-gain', we evacuated ASAP, dragging ourselves from our single but (usually) dual-occupied beds to spill out, shivering, into the freezing night air. The drill was to congregate outside our block, where we'd perform a sort of shuffling-on-the-spot dance, patting our hands around opposing upper arms, in an attempt to maintain some semblance of warmth. It was at this point that the skylarking and teasing would erupt – much cat-calling and mirth on discovering who was sleeping with who or who was caught in ridiculous jim-jams or various states of undress with mad bed hair waiting to resume slumber or, er, the activities that were clearly interrupted pre-alarm.

In second year we did psychiatric nursing. I was allocated to F block. Twelve challenging weeks of patients with cannabis-induced psychosis followed. There was electroconvulsive therapy (ECT) administered by the psychiatrists, usually in theatre, for depression. We would take the patient down to theatre and stay with them, so we witnessed the whole procedure. There were patients being tranquilised after significant threats of violence, naked patients running around the ward asking if anyone wanted to fuck and trying to get into bed with any or all of the other inmates.

I was once chased into a bathroom by one young man who was experiencing a cannabis-induced psychosis and an erection which he decided I should benefit from. I barricaded myself in and shouted for help. Help came and said chap was taken back to his bed. I believe he was sedated for a little while.

After several days, he was back to normal, though some weren't. He was the most charming man you could meet, polite, intelligent and insightful. The polar opposite of who he was under the spell of cannabis. I didn't ever believe that 'weed' was harmless after that period on the psychiatric ward, and still don't. There were so many that became someone and something else – both frightening to others and frightened of themselves. There doesn't appear to be much to commend it, and I speak as someone who tried it on one disastrous occasion.

We were sent out in the community on one module and tasked with joining an outgoing Jumbulance – a large passenger-type ambulance, not rigged up for emergencies, just for ferrying folk around and collecting the old people for the day centre. I missed my footing on the rear chair lift and fell with a hefty clatter onto the pavement. There was an assortment of gravel and stones embedded in my palms; I got up, dusted myself off, waltzed into Cissy's home and promptly fainted on her kitchen floor. She was waiting to be collected for her trip to the day centre.

I awoke to find myself flat out, on the multi-coloured plastic mat next to the sink, dress askew, knickers on show, staring at the baffled driver who was kneeling over me whilst Cissy, in her woollen coat and best slippers, leaned into her zimmer frame, slack-jawed at the drama unfolding on her kitchen mat.

Much mirth and amusement ensued amongst the oldies on the bus when we did get going, as we had to make a detour to casualty for a tetanus jab and removal of assorted stones from my hand. And all because the stupid bloody nurse had fallen out the back of the Jumbulance.

We decided that the elderly patients should have a ward party, as we were coming to the end of the secondment. The sister agreed that it would be fitting. There were a couple of crates of beer provided by Dad, a scratched Top of the Pops album was played loudly, followed by some Jim Reeves. Cans of pale ale were passed around and catheters bulged and leaked while patients danced and got merry. One chap said it was the best party he'd been to in ages and, poignantly, he died the following day. Just 24 hours before he had been swaying to T. Rex's *Ride a White Swan* with a tin of Watneys in hand. He had enjoyed one or two tins at most, but some would say that it was the Watneys wot did it.

*   *   *

Going into the third year, the white belts that we wore proudly were a sign we'd arrived. We got the opportunity to live in the West End, where Bart's leased flats for nurses' accommodation. We could choose Bryanston Square or Maybury Mansions, both in Marylebone, within walking distance of Oxford Street. I chose the latter and we availed ourselves of all that the West End offered – the restaurants, cocktail bars, discos.

There were gentlemen on the door of our accommodation by way of security to ensure our safety. Part of their role was to keep out our young men callers, who were not allowed to stay overnight. They had to be out by 11pm. The problem was the boys were already in, and staying in. Some of my fellow residents had become adept at using credit cards to open doors and slip them in and out of the building. When cleaners arrived for the morning shift the boys, who had of course stayed overnight, would hide in wardrobes or dodge round the corner of the corridor when security did the rounds – my boyfriend included.

Food often got nicked from our communal kitchen. I had only just purchased a chicken from Oxford Street M&S to be roasted in anticipation of my boyfriend's arrival. It was gone within minutes. I'd unpacked the shopping, then gone to my room and returned to the fridge to fetch milk for a coffee. No chicken. Bloody hell, that was quick! Where did that go? Was it passed on to someone else? Maybe there was an underground market for fenced second-hand chicken? But what I really wanted to know was, did they make proper gravy with the giblets? And if so, could they please get in touch to help me out on that one? Rubbish at gravy.

The block was later developed into luxury flats – not a nurse in sight.

40 years ago a nurse could actually save up on her earnings. I didn't consider myself badly off, even then. We managed to eat all world cuisines and drank the world's oceans dry. I took my first holiday to Italy having never flown before, and took trips to The Sanctuary in Covent Garden where we had massages, dainty snacks and sat on the same swing as Joan Collins, which hung over the pool.

We were invited to parties of friends of friends at exotic locations, like the town houses on Clapham Common, that I could only have dreamt of back in my freezing cold, lino-floored bedroom in Devon. Now I was partying with gals called Camilla and Diana, drinking G&Ts and hoovering up the canapés. It was in sharp contrast to life at home when I returned.

Mum and Dad had moved to a one-bed flat by now, which was brilliant because they finally had an indoor bathroom and lavvy. It not so good for me on my return trips, as there was no bedroom for me. Instead, a rolled-up sleeping bag and pillow were produced each night from behind the sofa for me to sleep in on the living room floor. (I'm quite tall, so the two-seat sofa was out of the question.) After a year or two, I think Dad was upset about the lack of sleeping arrangements and he applied for a caretaker position at an alms-house complex which came with a cottage for them, and it had – whoop whoop! – a second bedroom. Huzzah.

I undertook an eight-week secondment in theatres during my third and final year of training. There was a strict theatre sister who we all adored but who was clearly exasperated with the consultants, some of whom would shout and chuck their clogs at some lowly soul. She would frantically instruct us to make toast for them on arrival. 'Get them the paper – it's in my locker, butter them up a bit, make them coffee,' was the order.

It's funny, because although there clearly was a traditional hierarchy at that point, we felt that we all still mattered, despite the 'remoteness' of Consultants. I think we had more of an interconnected or symbiotic relationship with the seniors then, be it consultants or nursing officers, than we do now, to be honest. It feels that the whole of the NHS has fragmented more recently, and even the professional relationships we health workers have with social workers, speech therapists or GPs with whom we work closely are somehow more distant and, possibly, more fractious, as we struggle with limited personnel and resources.

Though there was the occasional consultant who would come in, open up the patient and then, pretty swiftly, leave. Off to the West End. Harley Street of course, and – though I don't know the specifics – it seemed likely they were still on NHS time. Their subordinates were left to finish up. One day, one such consultant was in the staff room. I had made him a cup of coffee and proffered the obligatory *Times*, trying to be as charming as I could, but then I thought I would toy with him, just a bit – ask him, why did they leave after opening up the first patient? Of course I knew the answer. Everyone did.

I looked him square in the eye and, with a serious gaze, asked as innocently as I could, 'Where do you go? Why do you come in for an hour and then leave?'

He spluttered and spat his coffee out in disbelief. I had put him on the spot and he now had to find the words to wriggle out of saying, 'I go up west to make a few bob on private patients,' without sounding like he was 'on the make'.

He hummed and hawed and transitioned to a very docile spaniel, offering a paw when begging not to be sent to bed in disgrace, muttering that it was 'excellent experience for the registrars to learn their skills independently – that is why they are left to get on with it. It's good for them. You know, they develop and become more confident.'

So I cheekily pushed a bit further and asked, 'Well, what do you do then? Where do you go? Do you work somewhere else?' I can't believe I had the nerve.

Again, there was panic in his eyes and he explained that, 'Yes, there are patients to be seen at other hospitals.'

'In the West End?' I offered.

'Yes,' he confessed. 'There are private patients to be seen.'

I had led him to where he did not want to go and he appeared chastened somehow. I departed with a cheery, 'Hope you have a great day, Sir, have to go – instruments to retrieve from steriliser.'

He expressed similar salutations, smiling weakly at me as it dawned on him – 'I didn't really want to have that conversation.'

Most of the doctors treated me well during my training, to be fair, including him. They were largely respectful and decent – the terror that was induced on ward rounds was largely an act. There were just a few who were completely patronising and condescending at all times but, very helpfully, not in any way discriminatory in their high-handedness – distributing it equally and with largesse.

There was a patriarchy at that point, to be sure. The consultants were usually male, generally privately educated, and were of a certain type – plummy rugger bugger types. They were hierarchical, usually quite disciplined and occasionally eccentric – such as those who always had a fresh rose in the lapel of their white coat or sported the clichéd bow tie. One donned a pair of leather gloves, which was an odd addition. Maybe he had his reasons – unsightly dermatitis perhaps, and trying to hide it? Who knows.

Any female consultant – and they were few and far between – was even more remote. They clearly had to be impenetrable and single-minded to attain that level of status at that time. I have to say though, they were largely well intentioned and, despite the theatrics of the ward round, where everyone stood to attention and wore an expression not dissimilar to those awaiting the guillotine, including the horizontal and bed-bound patients, most were absolutely dedicated, charming, hard-working to the point of exhaustion and decent people to the core. It has to be said.

The girl who lived in the opposite room to me at the Maybury was a total inspiration. Fi introduced me to *Fat Is a Feminist Issue*. Mind blown. She was funny, clever and self-deprecating. I had realised early on that I could no more be like the expensive gals than fly to the moon, but I thought

I could cultivate humour, and with my left-leaning politics I began to grow in confidence.

There was a rather grand if austere sitting room on the ground floor of the Queen Mary Nurses' building back at Bart's, all cream and green chintz, oak panelling and a stonking great grand piano, if you please, for practising your grade 8 if you were so inclined or talented – and some were. It was also a place to entertain your parents or an elderly aunt if they visited for the day.

Mum and Dad came up at the end of my training, for the qualifying ceremony at the Guildhall, in the City. There was a buffet, sandwiches and cakes and presentations of our badges and much joy, pride, applause and an endless list of double-barrelled nurses being read out. It was brilliant. We could now wear the long-awaited navy Petersham belt with our silver buckles sewn in, the sign of a qualified nurse.

Mum wore her fur coat. Dad wore a dark grey suit, blue shirt and navy spotted tie; on getting out of a taxi at Cheapside he was chuffed when quizzed by a passer-by if he was an MP. (That was when MPs had some degree of cachet, though. Not the charlatans that they appear to be nowadays. Some of them.)

* * *

I had fallen in love with London life. So, after qualifying, I worked as a staff nurse on James Gibbs ward at Bart's, an orthopaedic ward.

Here, I learnt to teach and advise other nurses and doctors – plus delegate, organise staff rotas, lead a consultant's ward round, manage others and be an all-round font of knowledge. One registrar decided that, as I had just come from running the male oncology ward on night duty immediately prior to qualifying, it would be safe to accommodate some cancer patients with us, so we ran the ward as an odd mix of part orthopaedic, part oncology for a while, when the cancer ward was full. I also managed to charm the ward sister and the nursing officer, something I didn't ever think I could. I realised that I had grown into a competent nurse and, as I gained the confidence to demonstrate that, my superiors responded.

When no one was around, the newly qualified SHOs would ask us, 'What do we prescribe for muscle cramps, say, for those who have had hip replacements?' They came out of medical school a little wet behind the ears, but some were savvy enough to ask for advice, ensuring they were well out of earshot of their peers or the dreaded consultants, of course.

There were elderly hip replacements, footballer's knees and ligaments, lots of traction for the broken bones, weights, pulleys, two-hourly pressure area care for sore backsides (bottom rubs with alcohol, essentially) and, rather wonderfully, our outlying oncology (cancer) patients, some of whom would beg to be readmitted to this quirky orthopaedic ward after having experienced us when there were no vacant beds on their specialist ward.

The senior registrars scratched their heads, smiling, puzzled as to why these patients wanted to be readmitted to us rather than their usual ward. The truth was that we seemed so much less serious, and even quite fun to those who had come from a ward where everyone was battling a life-threatening disease. It was relentlessly cheerful, with much teasing, football bants – I do actually understand the offside rule – and largely, and more importantly, nobody died. Well, rarely, on this ward anyway. There was still an unspoken understanding with the cancer patients that we were dealing with impending death; we just wore it more lightly and didn't surround them with that prospect at all times.

On the oncology ward, where I'd been just prior to qualifying, death was a common occurrence. However, on the other side of that ward, we dealt with medical emergencies. There was the admission one evening of an elderly chap with an aortic aneurysm that was likely to burst. Another had a dense hemiplegia – a one-sided weakness after a massive stroke – and he needed much care, turning frequently and hourly changing of bedding, as he was incontinent of urine. Another had overdosed on amphetamines, was admitted to us and sat in a side room with his feet in the sink, fretting and muttering incomprehensibly to himself all night. We just popped in on him occasionally to do obs and ensure he was still alive. It was early days in terms of my or anybody else's drug awareness. Largely in the 70s and 80s, booze was the drug of choice.

Our patients were suspended in the warm embrace of the 'cradle-to-grave' NHS, soapy bed baths in the morning, and sweet foamy Ovaltine at night. Sometimes, because the milk was cold for the last patient on the hot drinks round, a can of Mackeson's stout would be found. Yes, the NHS in 1982 ran to such things – each ward had an allocation of the stout, as it was seen as a medicinal (lots of iron in it) yet alcoholic treat.

There were the large wards with at least 24 beds, known as Nightingale wards, Dr Nelson's steam inhalations, intravenous chemo, sick bowls, medication for all ills, hordes of scary medics demanding X-rays, endless obs charts to be interpreted, the appearance of thundering steel trollies at meal times brimming with freshly made fayre, ever-present steel bedpans and tie-backed gowns – which guaranteed a glimpse of bare arse as the lads strolled to the men's room, to the sound of wolf-whistling from the others.

Big bosomed, bossy ward sisters, offset by fresh-faced, jolly nurses, joked with and teased the patients, which helped cushion some of these men, who were shadowed, skeletal, cancer-riven, from the terrible reality that they didn't have long to live. There were teaching sessions and handovers and allocations – we were purposeful, and happily so.

There were a few SHO's who we fell in love with. There would be talk of drinking at the Hand and Shears or the Bishop's Finger across from the main entrance. You knew from the chatter who would be there, so you might be tempted to go if a particular SHO or someone that you had a soft spot for said they were going. There was always somewhere to go and someone to go with. All this talk of being isolated nowadays and feeling bullied by social media would have seemed beyond alien then. We just got on, went out, did things – there wasn't much in the way of navel gazing.

The ward sister and I would nip to the nearby sandwich shop at lunch time to purchase crusts-cut-off, dainty smoked salmon and cream cheese sandwiches wrapped in greaseproof paper, which seems unbelievable now – I know! A lunch break!

Chapter Three
Babies by the Thames

I left Bart's in 1983 to pursue a new challenge. I'd enjoyed my second-year obstetrics secondment in Clapton, and I knew that I wanted to do more training and progress in my career. So I secured a place at the Olive Haydon School of midwifery at St Thomas' and Guys. I'd moved to south London, to Balham, and I felt more attached to the city than ever, so I decided to stay in the capital to deliver lots and lots of babies.

As part of our training, we had to undertake 40 deliveries, all of which had to be signed off by a staff midwife or sister. Of course, a delivery can take hours, so sometimes we stayed on long after our shift had ended to get the experience we needed.

We only truly know that everything is well when baby and placenta are safely delivered. Until that point, there's always the possibility that something could go wrong. As a midwife, this means there's a lot of scope for the unexpected. Fortunately, many women go into spontaneous labour and give birth 'normally' – or at least with little medical intervention. However, unexpected complications can occur.

One issue that midwives sometimes have to deal with is the cord getting wrapped around the baby's neck after the head has emerged. At the Olive Haydon School we learnt that, in most cases, the cord is loose and can be left or gently looped over the baby's head; sometimes, though, it can be very tight and, in these situations, we had to clamp it with two clamps and cut in between so we could deliver the baby's shoulders.

Of course I had to learn to do the dreaded episiotomy, though fortunately we didn't have to do it all that often – in cases of tight cord, an episiotomy would not necessarily be needed. It would depend on the perineal stretch, and so is often much less common in women who have already had children, who often have a more pliable perineum.

We learnt about shoulder dystocia – when one of the baby's shoulders is stuck behind the mother's pubic bone – and the series of manoeuvres which can be very effective in resolving the problem. We had to recognise an obstetric emergency, so we could call the obstetric team in when necessary. And we were taught all about the importance of examining the placenta to make sure it was all present and correct and healthy. Oh, and did the parents want to take it home to be eaten, as the new fad was then? (Some do placenta encapsulation now – getting it dried and made up into capsules!) There were notes to be written, tea and toast to be made for the exhausted new parents, beds to be cleaned and bin bags emptied. One minute we were expert midwifery practitioners, the next we were Mrs Mop.

As part of my 18-month midwifery training, I also had to do a community module to get experience of visiting mums-to-be and new mums on antenatal and post-natal visits to their home. I was allocated to work with an experienced midwife, Beryl, who was from Sri Lanka. She was very gentle and pragmatic in her approach to both mums and me alike. She wanted me to develop a sense of independent thought and decision making, so I was very quickly left to do the post-natal and antenatal visits alone, catching the tube and various buses around Waterloo, Stockwell, Brixton, Clapham, Oval and all points in between. She was a superb midwife and the font of all knowledge, nurturing but without being over-bearing. Beryl would chew betel (a leaf from an evergreen perennial, traditionally offered as a mark of respect or at auspicious beginnings in Asia). It's often used to wrap tobacco or an areca nut to add flavour. I could tell when she had partaken because her lips and mouth would be red the following day.

We ran midwifery clinics at Stockwell Park Estate, wearing the requisite white dress, turquoise belt and navy gabardine mackintosh with a navy pillbox-type hat in the community as a student midwife. The antenatal clinics ran on a Thursday afternoon and we, the student midwives, cut our teeth being left to organise these as well. Each expectant mum would have their blood pressure taken, we would listen to the foetal heartbeat, do the required urine testing, palpate the baby's position and ensure there were ultrasound appointments going forwards. If something was amiss, one of the GPs would be around to offer another perspective and maybe organise hospital admission. If, say, a client's blood pressure was elevated, accompanied by some visual disturbance, and protein in her urine was discovered. This would indicate pre-eclampsia and be considered an emergency.

After clinics we might pop to the shop, where the local confectioner had grilled off the entire display of sweets to disincentivise shoplifters. You had to make your Bounty bar purchase through a tiny, letterbox-sized gap through the metal grid. It was lively and a bit rough but, curiously, I always felt safe there. There was a Marks and Sparks within walking distance, where I sometimes bought supper if I was feeling knackered and had just been paid.

I carried a black holdall containing a Pinard's stethoscope, a sphygmomanometer and stethoscope for taking blood pressures. I also had swabs, suture cutters and the like. We visited new mums daily for the first 10 days after a normal delivery and longer if they'd had a C-section. There were the posh town houses at Stockwell to visit, where I would be invited to sit at the breakfast table with the entire family plus the live-in nanny for a 'proper' coffee if it was the first call of the day. Then there were families in the high-rise flats who were in close proximity.

There was a Traveller encampment at Vauxhall, which was difficult to access due to the dogs on the loose – obviously there to deter visitors. Once invited into the frilly, floral, knick-knack lined interior of the caravan, you would be allowed to weigh and check the baby in a rudimentary sense, but the Travellers were often guarded. They appeared to humour us and were not a little suspicious. It was rare to accomplish many visits to the families, as they were there one day, but gone the next. I remember trying to access one of the mums there as she had had a stillbirth, but she was reluctant to engage.

One dimension of the midwifery final examination in 1986 was the *viva voce* – Latin for oral examination – at Bonham Carter House, near Tottenham Court Road. The hall was filled with small wooden desks; on each was a number, a consultant obstetrician, a senior midwife and a vacant chair where we sat for our severe grilling on any obstetric topic of their choosing. We found our allotted table number amongst the hum of nervous chatter, hoping for someone friendly and approachable. Fortunately, I got both.

The consultant opened with a question about my breakfast. Disbelief registered across my face and the midwife began to chuckle. I thought it impolite to enquire as to why he was asking and responded that I had enjoyed egg on toast that morning.

'Yes, we can see that.'

I had a bright yellow smattering of yolk across my chest. Oh well, it broke the ice. I felt confident as we all smiled and romped through the breech deliveries, the manoeuvres that it necessitated, the episiotomies, post-natal depression, resuscitation of a newborn, pre-eclampsia and more. Yoking apart! He he! I hoped and felt that I had done well. And I had. Following the written exams, the practical assessments and undertaking the required number of deliveries, I became a qualified midwife.

* * *

I delivered hundreds of babies during the 18 months of training and the 18 months, thereabouts, that I practised as a midwife. And I think it's fair to say that being a midwife, especially on delivery suite, is a beyond stressful place to be. It can be overwhelming, and more so now, as staffing levels are depleted and many midwives have left the profession to go into health visiting – though that certainly has its own stressors.

One midwife I worked with would smell of booze when arriving on duty. She was very sweet but her tenure was very short-lived. Another would hide in the toilets if a 'crash' emergency C-section was initiated. I didn't get to either of those points, but I would sometimes catch the 88 bus from Balham to Waterloo with a very heavy heart.

There were endless obs, including blood pressures and foetal heart monitoring. There were epidurals to assist with and monitor, along with maternal blood pressures and vaginal examinations to establish the baby's position. There were amnihooks for the artificial rupturing of membranes, the fraught but quiet panic of meconium-stained amniotic fluid and foetal heart rates that didn't recover rapidly enough following a contraction, and then there were the quiet but steely mutterings of, 'We need to get this baby out now!' – usually followed by a crash C-section.

If we were dealing with private patients then the consultant would be more likely to do the delivery, but in the main the mums were NHS. Some were home births that hadn't gone to plan, and the mother had had to get to hospital quickly.

One such delivery has stayed with me. We had been alerted that Ellie was coming in after she had not made sufficient progress in her labour. If she continued at home, she and her baby would potentially be exposed to infection. I set up the delivery room in anticipation of her arrival with some degree of trepidation and anxiety. Though clearly not as much as the parents-to-be, Ellie and David, who traipsed in looking very glum indeed.

There is a huge amount of disappointment when your plans in childbirth go awry. Ellie and David had clearly felt that they did not want to be in a hospital environment for the delivery of their firstborn. That choice gives out a powerful signal. It essentially says, 'We reject the policies, procedures and staff – and we are willing to forego the usual services in order to do our own thing.'

After I set up a Syntocinon drip, used to speed up contractions, Ellie progressed, we chatted and seemed to get along well. I was always mindful that mothers may only get to do this once or twice in their lifetime, so each and every delivery is incredibly special and momentous.

Eventually, Ellie delivered in a kneeling position – which was quite unusual. In 1985, most women were strapped to a CTG to monitor contractions and the baby's heartrate, as well as the drip and delivery couch. I tried so very hard to provide the kind of delivery that they would have wanted at home – personal, relaxed, ensuring that they knew all of their options at all times. It was about striking the balance between ensuring the baby's safety and trying to let Ellie do whatever felt most comfortable for her.

They came in dreading the experience and, to be honest, I was too, as it's a tall order when you know that someone's expectations have already been dashed before you've even started. However, ultimately, in this instance, it was a bit like the party invitation that you really feel indifferent about – you go kicking and screaming to find it's the best thing ever, and everything about it exceeds expectations.

One year later, I was living in an entirely different part of the country, and a bouquet and a wonderful letter of thanks arrived on the doorstep of our fourth-floor council flat. That is why I love my job. All nurses and midwives treasure the thank you letters.

Essentially, a 'normal' delivery is such because it goes well. Everyone is happy and you feel relieved as a midwife. I used to think that I was only as good as my last delivery. It was a stressful occupation and still is, more so now, as the staffing levels appear to have deteriorated and I have heard that midwives are being asked to care for up to four or five women in labour at a time, which is wholly unsatisfactory, untenable and highly unsafe – it's also bloody terrifying. What happens if a baby's heartbeat dips for a prolonged period in delivery room one, but you are dealing with a similar situation in delivery room three? It really is life and death. You can only be in one place at a time.

The absolute worst part of the job was the disbelief and overwhelming sadness experienced on the occasion of a stillbirth. It was truly devastating. Claire came in at 27 weeks, having started contracting and bleeding. The baby had not moved for a while. I was relatively newly qualified and I felt completely overwhelmed by the emotion of the situation, all the while trying to project an air of completely calm competence.

Then, the heartbeat that had been there 15 minutes ago, now, inexplicably, wasn't there at all. The foetal scalp electrode (FSE) would normally ensure definite contact with baby's heartbeat, but it was now, terrifyingly, absent. Panic ensued for all of us, especially for Claire, for whom, until a few hours ago, life was bumbling along. She had been tipped from normality into quiet, agonising bewilderment.

The delivery suite was packed with all varieties of medics. After an abbreviated labour, I delivered a grey, limp baby and quickly handed him to the paediatrician who attempted resuscitation. Which failed, of course. The warm, lamp-lit, stale-air smelt of amniotic fluid and despair. Everyone was milling around, staring at each other, not knowing what to say. None of it made any sense at all.

The baby was returned to Claire after the paediatrician explained solemnly that, despite his best efforts, he could not revive him. The newly delivered mother gazed at her son, swaddled in the flimsy cotton sheet, and wailed. Claire had been through the agony of labour to no avail. It was the antithesis of what we were here for, wasn't it? This woman had been denied the fat, wriggling baby that she had lived for, hoped for and dreamed of.

I think it's fair to say we all contemplated giving up at that point. I went sick the following day and was called at home by the nursing officer. Reluctantly, I took her call. Remarkably kind, she took me by surprise: 'It is to be expected that we blame ourselves, but it really wasn't your fault,' she uttered, and advised returning to work ASAP.

I returned the following day with a heavy heart, but I knew then that this job wasn't for me in the long run. A baby had been lost and my thoughts were overwhelmed thereafter. There was always a bit of dread as I ran for the bus in the morning. This was an event that could not be un-remembered.

* * *

However, there was also something else that was weighing on me too, that made me not want to continue with midwifery. In truth, it was always there at the back of my mind, or the pit of my stomach. To be blunt, I'd had a 'termination' immediately prior to starting training, so had found myself in a surreal world surrounded by babies whilst tormented by the ending of my own pregnancy. I had wanted to be a midwife since the second year of nursing training, but there were still moments of harrowing disappointment with myself, and I felt wracked with guilt and wondering 'what if' most of the time.

It happened when I was coming to the end of my time at Bart's, having secured the place at St Thomas' and Guys. My boyfriend was a civil servant in the Ministry of Agriculture on Whitehall and had just signed on for full-time A levels at Southwark College, near Waterloo. This was Ken Livingstone's London, and the cost of the two years studying for A levels was the grand total of £1. We had decided that he should improve on his qualifications – like me, he had abandoned his A levels as a teenager some years ago.

He had been adopted as a six-week old baby – his birth mother had found herself pregnant and unmarried in 1957 – a timeframe with a whole different moral landscape. Whilst his childhood had been happy and secure, his adolescence had been more challenging. It transpired he was quite clever but his adoptive parents did not encourage or nurture that side of things. Dad was a sergeant in the Air Force and mum was a chambermaid. There are some parents who want the best for you, and others who feel a bit threatened by anyone, even their children, 'bettering' themselves. We thought it was now or never to make a future for ourselves.

We had just rented a flat in Balham with another nurse who we knew from Hackney Hospital. He was also heading south of the river, to work in Greenwich, so splitting bills and rent three ways made fiscal sense. While working my notice at Bart's, on James Gibbs ward, I finished a set of nights and was feeling odd. A bit sick, tired most of the time. I put it down to a particularly challenging run of nightshifts. But after a couple of weeks, I realised that I was also late with my period, so did a test and lo, the line was blue.

One sits mesmerised by the stick, staring, disbelieving, quickly turning your head away and back again. 'Maybe the line will disappear if I stop looking and turn back again quickly. Or maybe I need to look at it in a different light? Or maybe it's a false positive? Yes, that will be it.' So you do another one, but it's the same.

Much later, I did know the utter joy of seeing that blue line and feeling that full-to-bursting delight at two planned and much wanted pregnancies. But back then, as a newly qualified nurse and soon-to-be trainee midwife, it was too soon. We had no money to speak of, a recently rented Spartan flat with a gas leak, and my partner was about to give up full-time work to return to full-time education, supported by an evening job stacking pet food at Balham Sainsbury's. In short, it wasn't exactly the optimum time for parenthood – we were unprepared, under-resourced and overdrawn. Paying the flat deposit and keeping us afloat had used up much of my savings.

I remember making an appointment with occupational health back at Bart's, unsure about what to do. The kind doctor said that she would refer me for the termination, if that was what I wanted. I said I wanted a little more time. It seemed wrong that this should be a purely 'economic' decision. I was given one week, as I was around 8 weeks pregnant and the time limit was 12 weeks. I went home to see my parents in their one-bed flat, where I slept on the floor, as usual. So the parental home wasn't going to be a realistic option, for sure.

I trudged across to the council offices near my parents' flat and had a discussion with a man on the desk, which was highly unsatisfactory. When you are poor, you have to explain yourself to all and sundry, asking for help from total strangers. I think that's why I find poverty so bloody offensive; it's so intrusive. Poverty is having to ask others for permission to do things that those with resources can just do seamlessly. You make an appointment with the bank to ask for an overdraft, ask the benefits person for a claim form, ask the loans people for a loan, ask, ask, ask, please may I? It's like your very existence is an inconvenience – not just to you but to everyone else, so you should apologise and curtsey and tug your forelock. It feels like choice, dignity and opportunity are for everyone else. This was and is one of the drivers as to why I do what I do now. At least I have been there and can walk with you, advocate and understand.

Anyway, the guy in the housing office stared at me like he thought I had come from Mars. I needed some kind of connection with the area to be allocated a council property. I was born here, I explained again.

'No, I mean a recent connection,' he replied.

'How about that my parents live here and have done since the 1950s?' (It was now 1983.)

'No, you yourself, you, should have a connection.'

'So family and place of birth are not a connection?'

'No. You need a job here, something like that.'

'Well, I could get a job, if I wasn't expecting a baby, but I am, so that's why I need a home and that's why I am asking to be placed on the housing list.'

'Well, you can't be placed on the housing list. You haven't got a job here.'

I think we can see where this was going.

I wandered back to Mum and Dad's flat and passed what looked like some kind of municipal housing complex. I thought, well, nothing ventured, nothing gained. A man stood at his front door. I asked him how to apply for such a property. He said that you had to be elderly – it was housing for old age pensioners. I thanked him and decided to give up.

There was no way that we could afford to continue in London without immediate family who could help with childcare (we had none) so the only way ahead was a termination and me continuing the midwifery training. J. was returning to study in order to be the main breadwinner at a future date. This wasn't the time for us to be parents. I made an urgent appointment with the GP back at Bart's and told her I had tried to make things work, but it was pretty impossible. She agreed, and the referral was made for me to see a consultant gynaecologist at the Middlesex Hospital, Mortimer Street, in the West End. The hushed gossip was that the Middlesex girls came to Bart's for their terminations and vice versa.

J. came with me but waited outside whilst I had the consultation. Men were not party to such discussions at that point. It was a women's thing. He totally understood my decision and was supportive of it, realising too that we still had to make headway in a professional sense to make a life for future children.

I sat nervously in a corridor with other women. When I was called in, the consultant was diffident. He explained that he didn't like doing them, in truth. I kind of understood his position. Was there no alternative? I explained about my efforts to secure housing in Devon, the failure to do so, and hence my decision. He looked unimpressed and said he wasn't totally sold on the idea. Well, OK, but this is *my* life, isn't it? I had to explain about the lack of secure housing and how I envisaged being a parent, but not in these circumstances, at which point we had a somewhat tangential exchange during which he told me that he lived in the same part of the East End as me, and there was nothing wrong with *that* area. I narrowed my eyes and uttered words along the lines of, 'I might be stating the obvious here but, I think, just a little bit, maybe, just possibly, you just might be living in different circumstances from someone like me, what with your massive consultant's salary.'

I ventured that if I was fortunate enough to be allocated a council flat *anywhere* in London, which I hadn't been to date, chances were it would be on the 20th floor of a high rise, with lifts that didn't work. And isolated to boot. And that was if we were fortunate enough to be allocated such a property instead of getting stuck on a waiting list. He stared at me and booked me in for the following week. (Ironically, we did end up living in the East End, happily so, which is where we had both our children many years later.)

The law required two medical practitioners to agree to the termination so, to that end, a conversation had to take place whatever your circumstances, but having pointed out that I had no means to support a child and then to be contradicted by someone on a massive salary who felt that it would all be workable – *what was the problem?* – felt a bit demeaning.

On the dreaded day of the hospital admission, I shuffled along to the Middlesex with an overnight bag. J. came with me but I shooed him away after introducing myself to the staff and unpacking. One was not proud of one's admission to hospital under these circumstances. It was not a time to socialise with the person in the next bed or jolly along with the staff. It was unseemly. When asked, I explained to Lady in Next Bed that I was in for a 'minor op'. That much was true. I was not about to get specific, but people are often insensitive and she continued with, 'Oh, what you having, then?'

'Urm, a minor op,' I volunteered again, and turned away.

The staff admitted me, obs were done, and I received a standard NHS supper at the designated time – tepid and under the silver lid on a tray. A nurse came to talk to me about being nil by mouth the following day from midnight. I would be offered a gown and a pre-med at around 8am, something to sedate, prior to being taken down to theatre. Did I want a sleeping tablet to help me get some rest tonight? No, I'll be fine, I replied.

I wasn't. There were no mobiles then so I couldn't speak with J. and I didn't sleep much as I watched the clock in the Nightingale ward and listened to everyone snoring and the nurses padding around, diligently undertaking their tasks with the occasional creaking of floorboards, wishing I was on duty instead of lying here.

At around 8am two nurses descended on me. One was armed with the syringe and pre-med and the other with the gown. Curtains were pulled around my bed as though that magically rendered all conversations inaudible to everyone else's ear. Senior nurse asked me if my family knew I was here. I lied and said that they did. Were any family members going to collect me? No, but my boyfriend was. How are you going to contact him? I'll ring him on the wheelie payphone that can be plugged in next to my bed. They disappeared.

Then a lovely nurse appeared from the other side of the curtains, a vision of angelic blondness and empathy. She actually sat on my bed – no nurse sat on anyone's bed at that point in time, it was strictly forbidden for us to do so, but it was a very welcome gesture. The other two had stood over me, looking a bit embarrassed. She asked me how I was feeling. I smiled and said it was all a bit shit really. I was nervous and wanted it to be over as quickly as possible, now. She actually held my hand and said that it would be over very soon. She said that when I returned to the ward she would be on duty and would be doing my post-op obs. And she would bring me the phone to call J.

I loved that this girl, though still a student nurse, had the courage to go out of her way to make me feel cared for at such an awkward time, and I will always be grateful to her for her quiet thoughtfulness, compassion and defiance of the stuffy rules of the day.

When I came round after the procedure, the anaesthetist asked me how I was. Relieved, was my reply. She smiled a sisterly smile and whispered that she understood. I would be on my way back to the ward very soon as all had gone well. I saw the consultant later, who reiterated that, and then it was all over and J. came to collect me.

After leaving, we went to a nearby Wendy's – an American fast food outlet – for a coffee and sat and looked at each other. We had to continue with our plan now. J. with his A levels, followed by a degree, and me with midwifery. We owed it to our grown-up selves to make a success of things going forward. It's worth pointing out the most recent stats for terminations in England and Wales 2018: 24 per cent of all pregnancies end in termination, usually for socio-economic reasons.

I think it was then that I realised I was a feminist. A proper one. Not just a token one, using it as a label to appear fashionable or more substantial than I really was. A real feminist, overcoming female situations and obstacles. I was about to support another person, my partner, who had been dealt a real shit end of the stick due to his adoption, to better himself – we were going to make this work. I had to continue with this midwifery thing and continue to make the best of it all.

*   *   *

We settled in to our first-floor flat in Balham, and soon two doctors moved into the garden flat downstairs. We didn't know them beforehand, but being in the same line of business we soon got to socialising. One worked in orthopaedics, one in obstetrics. There were lots of rowdy goings-on, parties, BBQs. They always had the latest in gadgets and gismos – pop videos played on a loop to accompany their soirees and sound systems we could only marvel at, as well as the latest in all conceivable technology. We could stretch to a hired string of flashing lights for our parties and our cooker had a gas leak.

We had a disastrous and brilliant wholemeal pancake party one February. Bacardi and burnt batter. The guests included the usual assortment of pissed nurses in the midst of emotional break-ups, exhausted midwives and on-call doctors trying desperately to avoid the alcohol but easily avoiding the rubbery, grey pancakes. We even had gatecrashers who, inexplicably, located themselves on the 'free-range' top-loading washing machine (it shuffled noisily across the kitchen when in use). We had no idea who they were. They were drunk but good natured so we left them, happily, to the white goods.

We attracted a lot of waifs and strays whilst living there. Some whose relationships had irretrievably broken down came to stay and ended up not leaving. Some were friends of friends, some went to school with J., some he worked with. People slept on the sofas or the floor and when they left someone would take their bed or room. Effectively, we were running a hostel; we just weren't aware of it at the time.

I cooked an entire Christmas dinner, one memorable year, in a table-top rotisserie with half a door missing when the knackered oven fell into total disrepair. It was pretty decent, to be fair. Nigella, you would be proud. Only the roast potatoes let it down – they were a tiny bit hard. Well, the turkey was 'well done' on one side. And not *really* cooked on the other. OK, it was awful. The rotisserie had long since given up rotating, so I had to plonk everything on the base of this arcane Heath Robinson arrangement with just a single bar of electricity up top to heat the meal. I was on night duty over that Christmas period, so I was probably in a sleepless haze. It happens.

After completing that set of nights, I went home to Barnstaple to see my parents and J. stayed in London. One day he called to tell me that he had returned home to Balham from work to find the front door had been axed in. Destroyed. They were attempting to rob the downstairs flat. Well, we didn't have anything worth taking.

Another attempted robbery occurred some weeks later. I was at home and I heard what I thought was the 'boys' returning downstairs – a bit of door banging and heavy footsteps, some crashing around. Not unusual. 'Probably a few too many Harvey Wall-bangers,' I thought. Nope. Burglary. Again.

Blissfully unaware, I continued with *Only Fools and Horses* on the black and white, pootling around, whilst they got away with the downstairs sound system through the jemmied bathroom window. Ah, the joys of living within spitting distance of Bedford Hill, Balham, in 1985. I gather it's very gentrified now. Lots of chi-chi delis and cafés. The pinnacle of our sophistication ran to the Macky D's and a branch of Cullen's where we went when we wanted 'posh' cheese – i.e., not pre-cut and in cling-film – or some fancy ground coffee.

Back on delivery suite at St Thomas', crates of champagne would arrive after the safe delivery of a baby. Not every baby, of course, but lots of the clients were wealthy stockbrokers, bankers, that sort of thing. We would each be given a bottle to take home to accompany the inevitable Chinese takeaway, because getting home at 10.30pm, if we were lucky, meant no time to get creative in the supper department. After a late shift, 1pm until 10pm, I would catch the tube home, jogging into Waterloo, hoping the next arrival would take me all the way to Balham rather than the usual disappointment of 'Next train. 2 minutes. Stops at Kennington' on the dot matrix.

If I was on the early shift the next day, it inevitably meant an abbreviated and restless sleep, mulling over the day's deliveries after getting home at 10.45pm, knowing I'd be getting up at 6am before a quick strip wash in freezing bathroom, then donning the uniform and making a mad dash for the number 88 to get to Tommy's to do it all over again.

There were endless night shifts, sitting in the nursery at St Thomas', opposite a beautifully illuminated and mesmerising Palace of Westminster, feeding the babies who were on formula, listening to the tinny, irritating strains of 'The Birdy Song' ring out on the booze cruises as they drifted by on the Thames. That and 'Wherever I Lay My Hat'.

We would ask mums if they wanted their babies with them at night or have baby cared for by us, in the nursery, so they could get some sleep. Needless to say, there was nearly always a full nursery. Protocols and priorities are different now, quite rightly so, as we are aware of the need to breastfeed as soon as possible and have baby on hand to prompt and provide the cues, but that was the deal in the mid 1980s, and so it was no surprise that new mums opted for a decent night's sleep.

We would often gaze at these lovely sweet babies and wonder who and what they would become. Some were most serious in their demeanour and, after some deliberation, we would pronounce 'politics!' as their future profession. Some had an ethereal quality that could only be ascribed to an aspiring and burgeoning poet. We were amused to proclaim others as 'quite the intellectual' and felt sure that they were budding academics and philosophers. It tickled us to think of them as fully grown and in a professional capacity. With hair and a personality. Often their personalities shone through, even in those early hours and days. They really will be adults now. Yikes! Aged, ahem, 35! I wonder if some of our predictions were correct?

We could whip up a bra-top for mums whose breastfeeding boobs were painfully engorged using a bed draw-sheet and some safety pins. Ta-dah! A halter neck top to lock in the 'boobage' and render them immobile and 'contained'. There would be hot flannels, cold flannels and hand expressing of milk for their babies. If there was a surplus, it was to be sent to the 'milk bank' for the pre-term babies. Before a mum could leave hospital, we were instructed to show parents how to make a formula feed and demonstrate sterilising the bottles. We showed them how to 'top and tail' and how to bath their baby.

Staying on long after shift was supposed to end to deliver a client's baby was standard practice. Then we had to write up the notes and complete the register – an official document, kept in the delivery suite detailing the birth and associated information. We often taught new junior doctors some tricks of the trade, and then there were arguments with the very same (never with the senior ones, interestingly) about whose responsibility it was to clear away their trolleys and who was looking after Mrs So-and-So in delivery suite three. 'We're not handmaidens, you know,' was a frequent grumble.

* * *

After J. had successfully completely his A levels in maths, physics and chemistry, we headed back to Barnstaple. J. had applied to a polytechnic to do a BSc in computer science. This was 1985 and the future was computers, we figured. He definitely had the aptitude and inclination but until he had received his A level results, we didn't know if the poly place was secure. Meanwhile, I had secured a staff midwife position at the local maternity unit, so Barnstaple would be our base. We were going to get married too. J. had decided to make an honest woman of me.

They gave me the weekend off to get married in August 1985. The director of midwifery was cross that I hadn't informed her in my interview that I intended to tie the knot. I didn't know that I had to! There was no chance of my being a customer at the maternity unit: J. and I might have been sleeping in the same bed, but it wasn't at the same time. I had been put on three months of night duty! And, of course, it was the aim to push on professionally. J. had secured his undergraduate status and was driving 120 miles each day to Plymouth and back to his course at the city's polytechnic.

The majority of midwives were experienced and reasonably elderly, approaching retirement. One, I was surprised to learn, had delivered me, for goodness' sake. Miss A. was a bit of a battle-axe – well-meaning, unmarried and devoted to the cause, like most of them practising in that era. She was much 'afeared', as they say. I was bollocked often during morning handovers for forgetting whether a mum was breastfeeding or bottle. Tired and addled and coming to the end of three months' night duty, I hoped she might give me some latitude. But no. Stickler that she was, there was to be no sentimentality or forgiveness; we were all bollocked liberally and equally if she felt that standards had slipped. You knew you were in trouble if the half-moon spectacles were pushed down the nose and she peered over them to offer the steely gaze that penetrated your very soul as she sternly uttered, 'I see,' in a particular monotone. We knew what was coming.

We were all very fond of her despite her forbidding exterior – she was in possession of a sense of humour, though it was very well hidden for the most part. After getting to know you, she would refer to you as the hospital where you trained. On one morning after a particularly exasperating night shift, Miss A. grinned and proclaimed, 'You did well, there, Bart's.' High praise indeed.

I've often wondered if there is a special name for a group of midwives. A 'mirabiliary' of midwives as in 'miracle worker' – or a 'mabble' of midwives as in 'to wrap up or swaddle'.

There were babies named after us, there were babies born in the 'cawl' – the membranes – there were the hippy families who wanted the entire family present at the birth, which was never a popular request in the relatively conservative 'one person only' ruling of the maternity unit in 1985. I had to smuggle in members of one particular family so they could have the desired family gathering at delivery (there were elderly relatives, two teenagers and a toddler, all of whom were unexpectedly well behaved), but again I was on the receiving end of a bollocking for allowing such a crowd in the delivery suite when one of the seniors made an unexpected appearance. Oh well, it was the family's request. At least they were delighted that a safe and happy delivery had ensued. It's all that matters really.

But the Barnstaple midwifery job was just temporary. I was ready for a change and I'd decided to train to be a health visitor, but there were still a few months to go before I could start the course. I had secured my place at Plymouth poly and the funding by way of the employer, which was Plymouth Health Authority. The salary at that point was in the region of £8,000 per annum whilst training – the same as my midwife's salary – but, once qualified as a health visitor, it would increase to a starting salary of £10,500 (health visitors were on a higher pay banding than staff midwives).

My career was about to take off!

Chapter Four
Students Again

We moved to Plymouth just before I started training to be a health visitor in January 1986. I took a job on a care of the elderly ward as a stop-gap. I was happy to work on the elderly ward; it was a break from the day-to-day stress of delivering babies, and it wouldn't be for long. The move and working with the elderly was purely a pragmatic decision, as we were both to be based in Plymouth for the foreseeable future. It certainly made life easier (and cheaper) as it saved J.'s long daily round trip to uni.

We rented a fourth-floor council flat. This time, I had successfully argued with the council that we had a connection in the area: I had secured a job as a staff nurse at Mount Gould Hospital and J. was a mature student at Plymouth poly. Even then, the bloke at the council initially said we were not eligible. What is it with these people? First they say you need a job, then they say, well, having a job isn't good enough. I stayed and argued and then demanded to see his manager, who made an appointment to come and see us in the Barnstaple flat to discuss the possibility of a property in Plymouth. He came, and appeared quite serious and thoughtful. Then we were allocated 78 Castle Street, The Barbican – we hired a truck and moved in.

I encountered Fred and Clara on the long-term elderly ward at Mount Gould. They had been married for half a century. Clara had been a primary school teacher but now suffered with Alzheimer's. Fred would faithfully visit her twice a day, immaculate in collar and tie, diligently fussing over his wife, only to be met with such awful profanity from Clara that we all wondered how he stood it. 'You dirty mucker.' 'Arse arse arse unker.' 'It's in the effing cupboard.' They were all uttered like the most usual of phrases (not unlike Craggy Island's Father Jack).

Fred was keen to tell us how upright – the epitome of probity – Clara had been. Sometimes, not often, he would be embarrassed by her swearing, but we all knew his love outweighed any discomfit; he would have been lost without her presence and the routine of his beloved Clara's care – tenderly washing her, dressing her, feeding her her favourite tit bits, brushing her hair. She was like a baby bird, awaiting pureed spoonfuls which she gobbled up with relish whilst he wiped and soothed and chittered to her. He was truly a shining example of commitment and devotion.

There were others who shouted amusing nonsense randomly and repeatedly: 'Give me some cheese, you bitch.' Many were confused and needed dressing and feeding, trips to the loo and regular turning to prevent the sores, and there were those who were sadly sliding into their morphine-induced abyss and oblivion, the precursor to their demise. As a counterpoint, there were ice creams and jolly trips out to Cawsand and Freathy, Cornwall on the bus in the summer and, thank you so very much, there was no night duty! Huzzah!

The Barbican was in a lively part of Plymouth, by the water again. We lived cheek-by-jowl with the renowned Robert Lenckiewitz, a local artist who painted the famous Barbican mural. There was an abundance of pubs and eateries in and around the harbour, which was full of fishermen, builders, hobos, drunks (mainly students) and hen nights – take a look at any Beryl Cook painting. We were aware of her presence up on the Hoe. She would frequent the local bars to gain inspiration for her colourful and irreverent paintings of strippers or ladies in a taxi or having lunch, largely (and I use the word advisedly).

Cap'n Jasper's hot food takeaway by the seafront was at the vanguard of street food; here you could purchase a cheap, clear mug of tea – spoon chained to the counter to prevent the stealing of – and a 'marvellous mackeroll'. We paid our rent for our council flat in cash, in person, each Wednesday, at the council offices, with a rent book.

I commenced health visitor training at Plymouth poly in September 1986; the course ran for one year. We studied the principle and practice of health visiting, sociology, social policy and psychology, social aspects of health and disease and epidemiology, to name but a few components. We worked one day each week in a practical placement and spent one week toward the end of our academic year in an 'alternative' placement – mine was in Leyton, east London, as I had a friend, Sue, who lived there and kindly put me up. She was a health visitor, too. Sue was incredibly impressive and had an amazing work ethic. She really inspired me to want to return to London to practise as a health visitor.

But first there was a glut of exams, tutorials, plenary sessions, role play and plenty more besides to get through. We shared the core lectures with the district nurse students. We had projects to undertake regarding the holistic study of a family we were visiting, to include the family's journey, from antenatal, the birth, the post-natal period, the development of the child, the weaning process, the family's health, their mental health status post-delivery, other resources and services involved and much more.

The history of health visitors goes back to 1862, when we set up in Salford as an antidote to poverty and its inextricable relationship with ill health, morbidity and mortality, guiding mothers to the advantages of breastfeeding, immunisations, cooking healthy meals on a budget, ensuring good hygiene when making feeds, parenting tips and generally helping to create order out of chaos. Public health, clean water and sanitation were the most significant building blocks of the 19th century from which the health of the nation was built. But health visitors were there at the outset, before the inception of the NHS even, and, possibly, the Welfare State exists because of us.

During the 20th century, we were gradually formalised as a public health profession and service, moving into the NHS in 1974, along with district nursing, community midwifery and public health, which had previously been delivered through local government. Health visitors began to be attached to general practice, as opposed to operating out of our own clinic, and by 2000, this was the most common form of our service organisation.

My first placement was at Plymstock Clinic, a village to the south-east of Plymouth, but there was a problem. I should have learnt to drive, but hadn't; in fact, no female in my family had done so at that point. So I purchased a splendid bicycle, complete with front basket for my notes, books and lunch, for riding the four miles each way to my base.

There was always congestion at Vauxhall Street and Exeter Street, then there was the navigation of the dual carriageway – without a helmet, then, of course – toward industrial Cattedown and onward into the gently sloping village of Plymstock. I usually arrived red-faced with mascara everywhere, so a quick repair job was pivotal after each journey and before meeting Rose, my field work teacher, and the public. This was the start of my journey as a health visitor – it's one that has lasted these past 32 years.

We had a car ready and waiting for me to use – a pale yellow Triumph Herald saloon. It had a wonderful walnut dashboard and a little peel-back sunroof. It didn't have a working fuel gauge, but it had a switch in the boot to activate the spare reserve tank when we ran out of petrol.

I finally passed my test on the, er, fifth go. The manager at the driving school didn't bother asking how it went after the first two attempts. I was one of those deemed unteachable. I failed on something different each time and began to wonder, what was the point? I could clearly drive, technically, but on each test my head would implode and I'd lose my nerve.

On one test, the examiner made a lunge for the wheel as I accelerated out of a roundabout where, at all three junctions, all three vehicles had stopped. Someone had to break the deadlock, and I stepped up to the job! Oh dear.

Not the correct thing to do at all. That was attempt number two. I can't remember what went wrong on test number one. Everything, probably.

On number three I was wearing my nurse's uniform. While I was getting comfy in the driver's seat, the miserable examiner uttered, 'Don't think you're going to pass just 'cause you're wearing that.' 'I'll take it off then, shall I?' was my only thought.

Test number four, I couldn't parallel park. What was the matter with me? Of course I can parallel park. Just, seemingly, not on my fourth driving test. Fifth go, I bloody well did it. Yes! I kissed the examiner and returned to base where the test centre team waited expectantly for those out on tests to return.

I walked through the door looking faux crestfallen. The manager had that hang-dog look of despair, trying not to meet my eye, then I joyously announced my success. He breathed a huge sigh of relief as he hugged me. 'Thank Christ for that,' he muttered. I had seriously impacted the BSM pass rate, and not in a good way.

My rusty old Triumph Herald was teasingly called my 'vintage car' by my colleagues. Most whizzed around in the Ford Mondeo variety. There was an oil leak in the footwell, so invariably I had black oily patches at the heels of my shoes.

Back at Plymouth poly, we had dissertations to complete alongside the practical element of undertaking actual visits of real people and families. I endeavoured to learn and soak up as much advice and guidance as I could, and of course I read voraciously. I had learnt the art of study and revision from nursing and midwifery, and by now was adept at rustling up a cogent and well-argued essay complete with Harvard referencing very quickly. Sometimes the night before submission.

One day we had to present a seminar on health visiting practice to a public health consultant, who had dismissed us as 'nice gels' who were too unworldly to be familiar with gritty reality. Not sure where he got that notion from, but we disabused him of it pronto.

We did it in the form of a role play and dressed up in the clichéd style of prostitutes in order to shock him. I wore a short skirt with fag dangling from my bottom lip as we sashayed through a vignette depicting scenes of epic comic and calamitous proportions. Babies not being fed, profanity, ciggies with drink our priority, attending a baby clinic well soused.

One gal, Daisy, who had a nice line in understated irony, played the 'straight guy' beautifully – the quietly disapproving health visitor to the fictitious, chaotic and disorderly client. We had stereotyped wildly and inappropriately for comic effect. The lecturers were blissfully unaware of our goings-on and would have been furious had they known. The consultant admitted to having mis-characterised us as 'twinset and pearls', mistaking our reasonableness for being dull and naïve. He laughed loudly at our shenanigans and retreated with a very different perception of health visitors.

However, immediately prior to the session, I'd had to take J. to casualty as he had a football injury to his knee. He was brought home dangling between two friends as he couldn't weight bear. In casualty, post X-ray, which identified a dislocated kneecap, I had to expedite the application of plaster of Paris, saying, 'We've got to go. I'm playing a prostitute in half an hour.' They whipped up the gypsum in record time and we departed with J. inserted into the back seat of our yellow Triumph Herald, plastered leg neatly poking out of the front passenger window. Well, it was either that or the sun roof.

After a final training stage with our wonderful field work teacher, Jan, at Mutley Plain in Plymouth – she remains an inspirational mentor and friend today, aged 86 – I was finally qualified as a health visitor. However, I was not allocated a job immediately after qualifying. My bestie Diane and I were the only ones to be told we had to wait for a vacancy to arise.

How long was that going to be? I was the main breadwinner as J. was by now in the final year of his degree. We needed my salary as the car was only hanging together by a thread. There were monthly trips to the garage for numerous repairs. The bills were steep. I needed the new health visiting salary more than ever, if only to organise a newer and more reliable vehicle.

Diane and I were considered easier to hold at bay due to us having commitments in Plymouth – the others had no ties there, so they could have applied elsewhere for positions and would have been considered a lost investment. Management knew, however, that we couldn't move easily, so we just had to wait. How long for, nobody knew, and all the while those newly acquired skills would wither and perish, as would the motivation. Jan was furious. And let management know it.

I applied for a post in North Devon and started a few weeks later. It was such a relief to be commencing the job I had trained for and to put all that theory into practice. I could now upgrade to a brand-new red Ford Escort and I whizzed around Barnstaple and its surrounding villages, constantly honing and developing the skills and knowledge required for my new role.

*   *   *

As a newly qualified health visitor, one of my teenage mums told me that her latest boyfriend was flushing her toddler's head down the toilet. Mikey was 18 months old and being a bit lively; he also wasn't a great sleeper. There had been numerous bruises, some of which, especially below the knees in a mobile child, are pretty standard, but we discovered that some were on his ear and upper arms, which are unusual. His mum Crystal finally admitted that her boyfriend had been 'very physical' with her son.

After the initial shocking impact of her candour, I explained that this information had to be shared with social workers and that hopefully we would be able to assist her with a package of care to support her and protect her son. The social worker and I duly returned but – and there was a big 'but'– Crystal was now denying what she had said earlier. It was puzzling and exasperating – 'How can she deny what she had just told me only a couple of hours ago?' There followed endless meetings, telephone calls – no mobiles then of course – case conferences and home visits.

I had to continue visiting to support Crystal and Mikey but there was no change to the resolute denials that anything untoward had happened. I just had to keep going and offer other input to bolster the family, family support worker, help with a nursery place for Mikey and a speech therapy referral. I understood that Crystal had split up with the boyfriend now, but felt, intuitively, that there were others of a similar type who were around in the background. Because I was worried about her, I generally found a reason to visit her and offer support.

Some two years later, when I had moved to an entirely different part of the country, I was required to go back to give evidence in court, because there had been further neglect – and abuse to her subsequent children.

Whilst this case was sad, it was also comparatively unusual. As I settled into the job I got to grips with the routine and started to meet local families. Baby clinics were always a staple feature of the health visiting role. And there seemed to be more time to autonomously organise your caseload and work then. A big part of the job was the new birth visits, where we visited the family to discuss how feeding was going – bottle or breast – the importance of immunisations, how was everyone sleeping? Then we asked about mood and mental health.

We also did developmental assessments with the children. They were a more formal affair 30 years ago and were done at 8 months, 18 months, 3 years and then a pre-school assessment was made. There were vision tests at all these checks and the Oxford Drum at the eight-month check, where a child had to be seen to be following the diminishing-in-size dot which went from side to side.

The three-year vision check comprised another even more formal eye test – each eye was tested individually whilst the other was patched like a pirate. We used letters, or 'shapes' as we referred to them, for this. The child held a piece of paper with the 'shapes' on them and we would stand about six feet away with our lettered cards and ask if the child had the same 'shape' on their paper and could they point to it? It was also a test of comprehension and intelligence in being able to cooperate and respond accordingly.

There was a hearing test at three years for which we used a set of tiny toys known as MC Cormick toys, placed on a table in front of us. I would cover my mouth and ask the child to pass me the plate – there was also a plane so they had to distinguish between the two objects. It went on like this, with 'key' and 'tree', 'man' and 'lamb' and so forth. We tested each side, so I would move from the child's left to their right to see if there was a preference for one ear or the other, or if both were functioning well.

I loved the three-year check. They were always so eager to please and, if they were bright, they would question what I was doing and why, and just chat happily. There were colours to identify, could they thread some cotton reels, could they draw a circle? Pencil control was observed on this one; nowadays lots of children haven't been introduced to pencils due to all things computer. There was a book of animals to identify. And endless chatter as a result. Glorious.

With the parents I'd discuss preparedness for school; are they potty trained and dry by day? More recently, many children go to school in nappies, they cannot hold a pencil and might be speech delayed. We don't do a formal three-year check anymore which would have identified these children – it's just a cursory glance through the child's records to see if anything is amiss. But unless we have seen them recently, how would we know?

When I started as a health visitor, I would book a room in the GP practice and each child would have a half-hour slot. Parents would come religiously for their child development check. Now, we pretty much cannot find a room to book; if we do, there's generally an argument as to whether it's our day and, anyway, it's double booked and another team have got it for the morning.

We didn't just visit children exclusively in 1988. We also had elderly clients on our caseloads to access for health-related issues. One visit that stands out at that time was to a gent called Redvers. Redvers was a delight; he sat in his caravan, clad in his long johns, and tentatively asked about the potential for sheltered accommodation as the caravan got very frosty and the lavvy wasn't plumbed in. (Dickensian lavvies seem to be a theme with me.) There was a copper bed-warmer in situ and a wood burner. He held court, boldly adorned in a secondary pair of long johns on his head for added warmth and élan!

In our initial chat, I established that he had been in the First World War and was amazed to have survived. His older brother hadn't, which added to his air of sadness. After a few phone calls, some wrangling, a bit of haggling, a few letters and some further phone calls, I found him some local authority sheltered accommodation and we went to visit the centrally heated, all mod cons flat together. He had combed and slicked his hair; I suspected he had put in some teeth that I was sure weren't there before and he was in a natty, if ill-fitting, suit. I wedged him in the front seat, where he creaked and huffed and very quickly began to develop an unpredicted anxiety. We had a quick tour of the accommodation and the kindly manager said it was his, if he wanted.

But it quickly became clear that it wasn't right for Redvers. He shuffled and hummed and hawed and said he would give it some thought and we departed without a firm agreement. On our way back home to the caravan site, he started to articulate that he didn't really want neighbours or folk interfering. What was he saying? He already had neighbours. He didn't want to sound ungrateful, but finally confessed he was lonely and what he really needed was regular visits with an opportunity to talk to someone.

On facing the prospect of an overwhelming upheaval, he realised he didn't want to move at all. I deposited him at his freezing cold caravan and left him to disrobe from his finery while I cancelled the offer of the brand-new accommodation that had been extended. I continued to visit periodically, for as long as I could. We organised meals on wheels – which proved a hugely popular move – and Redvers did his thing. Largely sleeping and reading towards the end.

A year later, I was told that Redvers had had his lunch deposited by one of the meals on wheels ladies and she'd subsequently called the surgery to say she thought he didn't look well. The GP visited promptly and found Redvers slumped stiffly over his shepherd's pie and mixed veg. The steam from the buttered Jersey royals had created beads of condensation on his greying, pallid complexion. The sweet meals on wheels lady was right to be concerned. He really wasn't very well at all. Poor, dear Redvers was dead. He was such a blooming sweetie. RIP.

One of my stand-out visits in my first job was to a couple who lived in a coastal cottage. They had been married for some years but children 'hadn't come along'. The GP had deduced that they didn't know how to make babies, and it was my job to ensure that they did! It's almost unimaginable now to think that anyone could exist without being aware of sex, but without the internet and with no one advising you of the details, it was feasible. Unusual yes, but possible.

I visited over the course of a few weeks, late mornings; both parties were present. I was nervous. They were probably more so. Our training didn't quite encompass the sex therapist 'thang'. The first session was designed to make them feel at ease. I also had to establish if there was anything in their backgrounds that was affecting the issue. Both were from 'normal' families, it would seem.

I also had to grasp if there were genuine knowledge gaps, to understand their intellectual capacity, their perceptions and what they understood by 'making babies'. Was there something unpalatable about the act? Both looked nonplussed. They genuinely thought that babies arrived as a result of 'being married' and had no clue as to the finer points. I recall that there was mention of belly button sex but unless this lady had an umbilicus like, erm, a vagina, some information gaps had to be filled.

Fortunately they were at ease with themselves, and happy for me to ask impertinent questions. It took several weeks of treading a fine line in case I said or did something that induced the vapours or put them off for life. Teaching someone about sex is quite a responsibility. But very soon, within a couple of visits, the pair couldn't keep their hands off each other: there were offers of wine instead of tea – 'I'm driving, and erm, maybe, you shouldn't either... um, oh, OK, what the heck, you crack on.' (It was the 80s and we believed that Guinness was an obligatory health food in those days.) Two children followed in quick succession. So I think I did quite well there (she says buffing up her halo). Phew. Pamela Stephenson Connolly – you are quite the hero!

Sex is an all-prevailing theme in this job. Well, babies are the natural consequence after all, so it's blindingly obvious that sex is going to crop up, whether that's, 'How quickly can I resume our sex life?' to 'Is it going to be painful?' to a sheepish 'It's only a week after delivery; I wasn't expecting it! Can you organise some emergency contraception?' Lordy. Good for you, girl, and yes, of course I can.

I do recall a particular day when I became acquainted with the oldest profession in the world. Up close and personal. I had arranged to see an 18-month-old child for a developmental assessment along with his mother at their home. Pretty standard. I tried to park as close to the house as possible because I was carrying the obligatory scales and assorted toys, but there was a bloody great big articulated lorry which essentially blocked out not just all available parking, but all available light to the street too.

I knocked at the door. Dee opened it and ushered me through the hallway to the kitchen. I passed by the parlour room on the left, generally used as a dining room in the other terraced houses on the street. This one was clearly 'the boudoir' and was occupied by a double bed and a couple in the middle of, well, not to put too fine a point on it, shagging, and who were not going to cease their antics on account of me. A glance into the room revealed an old, balding guy with a fat belly gasping underneath a young brunette girl with her messy hair in an up-do, wearing a pink bra and not much else.

Dee laughed and attempted to close the door, saying, 'Don't take any notice of her – she's such a 'mare.'

'Should I leave? I appear to be interrupting…' I enquired.

Chuckling, Dee asked me to take a seat in the kitchen, which was just ahead.

At this point, toddler Anthony appeared, as Dee left, promising not to be long. The young chap was fishing through a black bin bag, ferreting for something. I thought, well, he's weight bearing and walking, his fine motor development appears good, he looks a decent weight, although I will weigh him to plot on the centiles. You can tell so much just by looking and listening to a child.

He approached me with a big snotty smile holding a magazine, which he proffered up to me as though this were the most usual thing in the world. It was a copy of *Razzle*. Dear Lord. This 18-month fella has a job. He chattered away to me in that toddler, polysyllabic babble. Speech is OK, I thought.

I heard the proceedings come shuddering to an audible halt in the next room. I wondered if it would be impertinent to ask if these events were usual but I concluded that they probably were, so no need to ask...

We would definitely be viewing things through a different lens in today's climate, but Anthony appeared loved and happy. He was probably a maths expert, for goodness' sake. Counting 10 pound notes, perchance? He was an entrepreneur in the making. If I failed him then I am guilty as charged. I have visited much, much worse, believe me, M'Lud.

* * *

I have had the good fortune of meeting some fine practitioners in health visiting through multiple and hugely diverse training sessions over the years. There is and always has been a vast array of training on offer in health visiting, not only because it's important to be up to date with the latest legislation and thinking relating to our work, but because there is a lot of independent assessment and thought and judgement involved in being on one's own in a family home, and having to make the right decision and do the 'right' thing, that can potentially have far-reaching consequences. Be it undertaking a hearing test, assessing safe sleeping for baby, referring to speech therapy or having a fractious conversation about why you now need to involve social workers.

We studied the dynamics of relationships by way of something called 'One Plus One' training, an introduction to relationships course for professionals, to help us to assist with issues surrounding crisis points in a partnership/marriage.

The Children Act of 1989 was passed not long after I became a health visitor. Prior to this act, dealing with different aspects of childcare law was lacking in coherence. The new legislation provides a 'toolkit' to find a fair outcome for children. The Act ensures the safeguarding of children by managing local authorities, courts, parents and other agencies, prioritising the child's wellbeing, health care and human rights. There were and are multi-disciplinary training sessions, gathering together social workers, doctors, midwives and teachers.

We had regular and mandatory study seminars regarding breastfeeding, first aid – both adult and paediatric – managing conflict and fire training. We even had some self- defence training when we were student health visitors. There were continuing child development updates, 'smoke stop', carbon monoxide training, mental health updates and plenaries, amongst so many others. There were also complimentary calorific breakfasts with formula milk reps – strictly *verboten* now, for fear that we may be tempted to promote a particular brand of formula depending on who had fed us or given us a pen.

One of the 'analytical and critical thinking' sessions that has guided me and underpinned much of my decision making, especially with regard to safeguarding, was the one on psychologist Edward De Bono's technique of 'six thinking hats'. De Bono outlined the six 'hats' that we wear when trying to make an appraisal that, when used effectively together, can aid us in good decision-making and improve our judgement skills.

The white hat calls for the facts. Just the facts: what do we know for sure? The yellow hat represents brightness and optimism; when wearing this hat we explore positives and benefits and the value therein. So, in a child protection scenario, we consider any tangible good things that are demonstrated or in place: a parent who prioritises their child's needs above their own when there is a crisis, demonstrating love and warmth when all around is falling apart.

The black hat represents judgement. Why may something not work; what can you see might go wrong or be difficult, or where might danger lie? That might be where we think about 'what if' scenarios. What if we leave this child in this house where there is constant chaos, firearms, drug-taking?

The red hat denotes feelings, hunches and intuition. There are times, especially as an experienced practitioner, when you intuit or interpret what is going on. Professional intuition is something that takes years to develop. It is a dynamic process of reflection combined with, 'I have seen this before', synchronised with 'How do I process this and what do I do with this now?' It happens in a split second, usually. It is not used as an isolated 'hat', of course, but in conjunction with all the others. You can express emotions and share fears, likes, dislikes, loves, hates – but these should all be moderated by the wearing of the other hats too. We are not there to express untrammelled emotions, but to put things into perspective. The black 'judgement' hat blends into this one – what might be the possible outcome if we do nothing when faced with a particularly worrying situation?

The green hat focuses on creativity, possibilities, alternatives and new ideas. Is there another way of looking at this situation? This problem? This child? There needs to be an opportunity to discuss new concepts and perceptions. In this scenario, a health visitor, in conjunction with social care, might need to consider bringing in, say, a family group conference, whereby the whole family support network might be brought together to discuss and thrash out ways of supporting a particular family to avert a crisis. Or it might mean applying to a charity for an item that would solve a problem previously considered insurmountable, for instance. Or it could mean referring a mum for an assertiveness course or similar.

The blue hat represents the thinking process. This is the 'control mechanism' by which the six thinking hat guidelines are observed. In other words: have I considered everything?

One ordinary rainy afternoon, I was sat in reception at the practice, chatting to the receptionists. It was quiet and almost 4pm. We were chattering about nonsense, inconsequential stuff, waiting to go home. The phone rang and it was one of my clients, Sandra. She wanted to speak with me. She was mum to Ellie, aged 12 months, and she said she didn't want to be a mum anymore. Okaaaay – on my way.

It might be useful to explain, as it might not be clear, that our clients are referred to us initially by email (these days) from the child health department, either following their birth or if a child moves into our area. At this particular point in time, decades ago, we received a hard copy of the birth notification through the internal post outlining the birth details. Sandra and Ellie were hence known to me, and had been for the past year.

Sandra had not bonded well with her daughter. She wasn't enjoying any of it, she told me. Nothing. A day hadn't gone by when she'd not thought it had all been a mistake. This was the first time she had shared this with me and, in truth, there had been no 'red flags'. There wasn't much in the way of extended family support and she missed her social life. We talked about ways of trying to make things work. She could attend groups, I would visit weekly to talk about how she was feeling. We would make an appointment for her to see her GP. How else can we/I help you to do this? We had a long chat. My side ran along the lines of – you'll change your mind.

'Perhaps you want to go out this evening, is that it?' I asked.

'Well, yes, it is,' she replied, 'but I have been feeling like this for ages now. It's not new.'

Sandra begged me to take her daughter. Literally begged.

'Where to?' I asked. 'Can't you talk to family or friends to make arrangements, just for tonight? You can then go out and have a good time but not go through with this rupture of such magnitude.'

'No. I want you to take her. I don't have any friends or family who will help. I would have called them if I had.' Sandra was adamant. There was no dissuading her.

'OK, I'll call the social workers and see what they suggest.'

I spoke to a social worker who was up to her eyes in another situation; she advised me to take Ellie to the local hospital. It was beyond miserable. This little person had no clue as to what was about to happen. I placed her on the rear seat of my Ford in her car seat. Sandra wanted to give me her clothes. I took a carrier bag full. And the last of the formula milk. I asked her over and over and over if this was what she really wanted and yes, yes, yes. It really was.

A staff nurse on the paediatric ward at the North Devon District Hospital was expecting Ellie, as the social worker had called to pre-warn the ward. I handed her over – she didn't cry and wasn't in the least bit bothered by the new people or her new surroundings, which was quite telling. The comforting nurse hugged her and Ellie remained solemn but unperturbed. The nurse took the clothes and the formula milk. I explained the situation again, almost disbelieving of it myself. There was nothing else to be done, so I had to leave Ellie there.

On the following Monday, I called on Sandra. She said that she was absolutely fine, she didn't want her daughter to be returned. A foster placement was found very quickly for her. Sandra didn't ever change her mind and Ellie was, thereafter, put forward for adoption.

I have gone over this scenario repeatedly in my mind for a long time afterwards and wondered if there was anything that I could have done differently to keep mother and baby together. Perhaps she had been unknowingly depressed – well, of course she was – and this was a 'blip'? Perhaps I could have persuaded her more convincingly that this was a mistake.

But then I realised that it was not my decision to make. It really wasn't about what I could or couldn't do. It was about Sandra and her capacity, at that given time, to parent her daughter, and effectively so. She had made the decision that she couldn't do it. It was true she didn't have any support-ive family, and often they can and do make the difference

– it's lonely and beyond difficult on your own with no respite. Perhaps, it really was best for the both of them.

It should be noted that this event took place back when the entire child protection framework and landscape was of a completely different hue. We were operating at a time when if a case conference involving the different professionals working with the family was convened, the parents were not even invited and would be informed of the decisions and plans after the meeting had drawn its conclusions, which seems utterly alien and preposterous now – but it really was the way things ran then.

* * *

Most health visitors go back to the office and think about you. We have to write up an account of our visit, what we observed, what was going well. But we also might worry about you at 3am when we are up for a wee. Is there another agency I should involve or refer to? Do you need money, friends, family, do you need to go out more? Go out less? Especially if drink and drugs are involved, and they sometimes are. And if they are, can you prioritise your baby's needs over your own? How are you handling the baby? Is there a partner ever present when I visit, monitoring the conversations, guarding the situation in case I get to know too much?

Worst case, after a visit, I might need to pick up the phone to a refuge to organise a place for someone escaping violence, or contact social care because we are unsure as to how this non-mobile baby got a bruise on his face. Perhaps it's evident that there's not enough money for groceries, and I'll need to organise a food bank voucher.

Often when someone requires a food bank voucher, it's the tip of the iceberg, as there is so much more going on. The food bank contacted me recently to let me know that a client had dropped her child off at school, went to get petrol, but her debit card was declined and so she could not collect her child from school at the end of the day. Understandably there were tears of frustration and anger as to how her life had got to that single point of failure, as she saw it.

I drew out £30 (I do try not to give clients my own money, but sometimes there's nothing else for it) and drove to the food bank to give it to her for petrol. Meanwhile, the food bank sorted her out with comestibles for a week. She was not actually my client, so I left an urgent message for the health visitor concerned to follow up with this lady. I never knew how her life went thereafter.

That's how it goes. Whirling into episodes of crisis and out again.

Chapter Five
That's Dad, By the Way

J. graduated and got a job as a programmer at a defence company in Barnstaple. But there appeared to be little work to do. The highlight was sometimes guessing the time that the lights of a nearby motel would be switched on. So, as there didn't seem to be much of a future there for him, we took the decision to head back to London. At least there would be a range of employment options available to him. I think I was a bit ambivalent, initially, about the return to the city, as I was happy in my work at my current surgery and envisaged our future in North Devon, but it wasn't to be. Although there was part of me that wanted to test if I could 'cut it' in London as a health visitor. So off we went, again.

I secured a position in Stoke Newington in January 1989, which was just as well, as J. was starting work as a programmer at an insurance company near Holborn at the same time and we had a couple renting our one-bed house in Devon. We had also purchased a flat in Hackney and were due to move in at the same time as our new employment began. Everything happened at once.

We were yuppies now, allegedly. But the flat back in Barnstaple was a nightmare. The rent we received didn't meet the mortgage repayments. Not ever. We were always, without fail, at least a hundred quid down and sometimes, if someone had moved out and there was an empty spell, were paying two mortgages. And that was often. The tenants came and went remarkably quickly.

As soon as we moved, interest rates sky-rocketed. We felt comfortable for all of our first month back in the 'smoke', then it went pear-shaped. I developed a form of stress-induced acne which took months to get under control. This was to be our first experience of an economic recession, but not our last.

My new post in Stoke Newington meant adapting fast to the many different family situations I would meet in the area, from becoming acquainted with the Hasidic community and understanding the importance of Shabbat and, hence, avoiding visits on a Friday afternoon at the lighting of the candles, to finding myself in a squat where there was no running water or electricity and a 10-day-old baby to attend.

I witnessed, first hand, the Poll Tax riots. I happened to be gazing out of the barred windows of the health centre at Lower

Clapton awaiting my family planning appointment. Getting the diaphragm checked or something. Anyhow, there was the sound of something unrecognisable and slightly sinister. My ears pricked. A crunching, rhythmic sound. Getting louder and closer now. A veritable army swung into view marching from Urswick Road onto Lower Clapton road. Police, dark uniform, visors, shields, batons. I watched the surreal and not a little scary spectacle open-mouthed, rooted to the spot. They moved resolutely and as one, stomping to the town hall where it all kicked off for the whole country to see on *News at Ten*. Horses, the riot police, angry hordes. The whole clashing caboodle.

Watching the telly in the comfort of our sitting room that night, we could hear the shouting and rioting in stereo as it was unfolding only yards away outside; we were terrified it would spill over onto our street. Oliver Letwin's brilliant idea, that one. As one wag observed, 'Is there nothing that he can't make worse?'

* * *

We had been back in London for a year when I found out I was pregnant – and happily so. It was planned and much wanted. I was beyond excited at the blue line on the pregnancy test on this occasion. I carried on working until about 36 weeks and began collecting all the necessary items for him.

I used to sing to him during pregnancy and imagine what he would look like. On a bright February morning I went into Homerton Hospital to have him, by an emergency-ish C-section as it turned out. I got to 9cm but failed to progress thereafter – anterior lip of cervix got in the way of a normal delivery. He was not in distress and fortunately we had time to pop in a 'spinal', as we called them, so I was awake to hold my Beautiful Boy (BB) on arrival.

Ridiculously, J., who was in the theatre for the momentous event and wearing scrubs and the blue shoe covers, got mistaken for a medical student by the scrub nurse, who collared him and asked him to open a suture packet onto her trolley. As this was his first time, as it were, he looked at her blankly, which further infuriated her, as she barked again to open it up. He picked up what she thought she wanted.

'Yes, open it and tip it onto the trolley,' she reiterated.

Still thinking that this was a new and inclusive thing – 'This must be how they get dads to be useful in the process,' he thought – he stared back at her, wondering what else he would be required to do. It was only when a saintly student nurse piped up, 'That's Dad, by the way,' to the scrub nurse, that he got 'relieved of his duties'. Profuse apologies were extended and he got to sit down with me at the head rather than the business end, for which he was even more relieved.

On the post-natal ward, I recognised a middle-aged Salvation Army midwife I'd worked with in my student nurse years at the Mothers' Hospital, Clapton, 12 years earlier. I had clearly not made an impact as she didn't recognise me, nor was she terribly complimentary on this occasion. She was at the nurse's station talking with a physiotherapist and I was wandering around only a few hours post C-section, bent over and slowly shuffling along, pushing my IV stand and holding the wound drain. I didn't possess a nightie and so I'd donned a long t-shirt. I heard her loudly proclaim to the physiotherapist, 'She's a health visitor, but you'd never know!'

Bloody cheek! I remembered her as being unsympathetic to mums at the Mothers' Hospital when I was a student, so I felt that it was a badge of honour to be slighted by the disapproving old bat. I never did get the nightie thing. Well, we were all girls together, weren't we? I wasn't used to being on that side of the bedclothes and I just didn't think folk would be so judgemental. Nurse! Get me a full-length nightie, long of sleeve, and pie crust of collar, stat!'

I was beyond happy to gaze at my Beautiful Boy in his 'Froggie goes-a-courting' suit. It was the first thing he wore. Luminous green with bright pink spots. I was determined not to be the pale-blue-knitted-cardie sort. He breastfed very readily and soon after delivery, so I thought I had it cracked. Not so.

He resolutely refused to wake for ages due to the Pethidine (pain relief) administered to me immediately prior to the C-section. He continued to sleep even when the photographer arrived the following day and tried to 'arrange' him for the session. Nothing fancy, not like nowadays, where they are placed artfully in plant pots (maybe when they're a bit older) and the like. Just a full-frontal fully asleep pose. He was bright yellow but, thankfully, not jaundiced enough to need phototherapy (ultraviolet light).

While the midwife seemed happy to pronounce on the calibre of my character on account of my deficit in the nightie department, she didn't offer any help or advice with regard to breastfeeding and getting Beautiful Boy to attach. He fed sporadically after the first day, and I realised it wasn't a done deal that this breastfeeding thing was going to work.

I thought that home would be the best place to work this out, so I discharged myself on day four. I didn't really relish the disapproving demeanour of said midwife, plus I was an unwilling audience to all the public and heartrending telephone conversations on the huge, wheelie, coin-operated, plug-in phone at the end of my bed. 'Allo? Yeah, I've 'ad 'im. Yeah, he looks like you. Are you comin' in? Well, when then?'

Some mums were well and truly on their own, and how bloody hard that was going to be. I wanted to go home to my own bed and bathroom and be a mum on my own terms.

There was, however, a wonderful cultural and culinary bonus in being an inpatient for those few days: a Bangladeshi mum was in the next bed with her newborn. Her family came to visit armed with all manner of delicacies and curries which she very generously shared with me. Apart from J., who was at work all day (he was self-employed as a programmer and wouldn't get paid if he didn't show) and so wasn't about to whip up a chicken jalfrezi, there were no family members who could get to me, so I was immensely privileged for those few days to be included as if I were a family member by my friend in the neighbouring bed.

I landed at home on day four and the midwife arrived on day five. I was in a mess. Was I breastfeeding or formula? Technically, I was both, as BB was still sleepy and appeared to prefer the bottle at this point, but I was still shoving the boob his way, in the vain hope that he would take it as he had on day one. The guilt and sense of confusion and failure prevailed, as with all new mums. We woke during the night – the boobage was Dolly Partonesque. Sitting up in bed bedecked with a tiny string of white lights, which enabled us to make up a formula feed with the kettle on the floor.

Formula was all he would take until ta-dah! The midwife who arrived the following morning sat me down, placed her hands on my shoulders and said, 'You need to lend yourself to daytime telly, sweetie; it's what it's for. New mums need entertaining.' My shoulders dropped about five inches. She continued with, 'Let's give him another try on the boob – he looks like he's woken up a bit.'

There was a bit of fiddling and faffing – we had to get the areola (brown bit of the nipple) in, gently encourage BB's chin in a downward trajectory, mouth gaping, and lo! On he went. He fed like a very hungry caterpillar! Starving one actually. On Monday he fed on one boob, on Tuesday he fed on two. You know how it goes. The latch, all puffed up cheeks, the chomping, the audible swallowing and fishy pouty lips, and the sense of connection and achievement – we could do it, after all!

I endured a couple of bouts of mastitis followed by appropriate antibiotics and we sailed on, but it has to be said, it wasn't easy at all at the outset, which is why, even as we encourage and promote breastfeeding, we have to be incredibly sensitive to everyone's needs, preferences and support the decision that each mother makes. It has to be right for them. If a mum has decided that formula is the way ahead, then that's the direction of travel, no ifs, no buts. We support your decision-making.

We had a wonderful three months together. With BB in a Baby Bjorn sling, we went on the bus to all manner of art galleries and exhibitions. I had coffees out and met friends for lunch. Occasionally I would meet up with Fi, who had lived opposite me at Maybury Mansions – she was also resident in Hackney and had a baby boy, too.

Those precious three months went quickly, and then it was back to work. I had to find a childminder. The mortgages had to be paid. How hard could it be? I mused. Turns out so much harder than you think. The first place I looked at, the lady in charge turned out to be an ex-colleague. 'Hello Fatty,' was her greeting. Nice. I wasn't sure if it was me or BB or both to whom she was referring. I went through the motions of being interested whilst being shown around, but I had immediately discounted her.

Then there was word of a vacancy a few streets away. This looked promising. The other mums who formed her client base seemed quite normal. She was expensive, however, but that was how it was. We accepted her kind offer, and so I returned to work reluctantly and BB went off to the childminder with an accompanying letter outlining his preferences and dislikes. The note concluded with tear-filled, plaintive, 'I hope you love being with him as much as I have done.' Lots of mums get teary at the return to work. And there are plenty more tears thereafter. Oh yes.

We were over our overdraft limit most months due to high interest rates and the other mortgage to pay. Often we had to negotiate with the bank each week to pay the childminder.

I would phone in my lunch break at home to do the usual pleading. There were tears every Friday. But overdraft was usually extended.

Interest rates were at over 15 per cent! So our planned outgoings had doubled in a very short period. Major and his grisly gang really screwed us over. J. or I would draw cash out and jog back to work and then, on completion of the working day, collect BB and pay the childminder the 'cash only' that was stipulated. The other mums who shared childcare with us thought that I was odd and didn't really get me. No wonder really. Grinding out every day knowing you can barely afford to is overwhelming. They were lovely and professional mums too, but clearly not in the same situation as us.

One fateful day, I called one of them regarding a social event that we couldn't attend but, coincidentally, she wanted to speak to me. They all wanted to give the childminder a pay rise, and asked if I would be happy to go along with the suggested sum, another £100 per month. Oh joy! I couldn't contain my lack of enthusiasm and said something like, 'Oh well, what's another hundred when you haven't got it?' It wasn't long before we parted company with the child minder, as J. had a subsidised day nursery place offered at his work. We practically jogged over to the nursery, where we eagerly accepted BB's place.

At the weekends we'd often escape to the seaside. Burnham-on-Crouch. Walking by the river always felt so calming in a way that you couldn't feel in frantic Hackney. There were frequent threats of bombings and there had been one at the Baltic Exchange. I worried about J. as he worked in close proximity to the City. Then there was the attempted bombing of Canary Wharf. The windows of our Hackney flat shook for a protracted period that evening, accompanied by the loud explosion. Definitely a bomb, we said, as we met each other's gaze solemnly.

I had loved London over the years but now, with a child, I found it hard-edged and lacking in family friendliness. Although it has to be said that our neighbours in our street were very dear – we were lucky that there was a real community there. But I was beginning to tire of the struggle – financial as well as in every other conceivable way.

* * *

I was getting into the swing of my return to work. One day I visited a mother who had recently been allocated a council flat with her new baby and, shockingly, on moving in, she had been met with a floor-to-ceiling giant black swastika adjacent to the open fireplace. I often wondered which idiot previous tenant had painted that monstrosity. And why. This particular feature wall wasn't likely to feature in *Country Living*.

I visited weekly, mesmerised each time by this unholy décor. I think I tried to get some money from a charity to help with decorating, but to no avail. It was about this time that councils were refusing to renovate prior to tenants moving in, so this new mum had to live with said swastika until she could afford a paint job. She did so well with her lovely baby – that was the main thing, despite the hideous motif.

There was such a diverse mix of clients to get to know and love. There were gals who used clingfilm instead of condoms when 'in extremis'; there was the HIV-positive lady who entertained clients at breakfast time, Special Brew on the go at 10am. AIDS was of course the big public health concern of that era. Her refugee status meant she was in receipt of reduced benefits, so she became a prostitute to augment her meagre income. I used to take her condoms, but she said she could charge more if they were not used. I took them all the same...

I'd only just returned from maternity leave and was still breastfeeding when I sat down at my desk one Monday, opened one of the many letters stacked up there and, crestfallen, discovered I was due in court back in Devon that very Friday to be quizzed about Crystal and Mikey, who I had visited some two years ago. Oh joy!

I telephoned the eternally jovial county solicitor who greeted me with a 'What ho, Rachael!' Cut with the jollifications, Mister; I am not best pleased. I pleaded with him not to make me attend. Don't make me. I can't. I won't.

'What happens if I don't turn up?' I asked him.

'I'm afraid you have to. You would be subpoenaed if you refuse.'

And so I was. A leather-clad courier came to the health centre and handed me the bloody envelope. Damn. I had to go.

So, the day before I was due to give evidence, my three-month old baby boy and I waved faux jovially to my husband at Paddington Station to head several counties and 200 miles away. I had to take BB because he was still largely breast-feeding, even though I had returned to work. If I had left him with J. he would have been too upset, and I already felt guilty in returning to work and leaving him. J. was still self-employed at this point, and due to our financial pressures, losing his daily fee for work was just not an option. So off we went.

I wore BB in the Baby Bjorn carrier, leaving my hands free for the overnight bag. The first question was: how do I breastfeed while sitting at a seat pressed so close to the blessed table? I couldn't actually get him in front of me to hold him properly. Maybe if I twisted side on to the window… Yes! I can do this.

I can't remember if I needed a wee on the train. I can't have done. Where would I have put BB? There's no room for a full-grown person in those tiny cubicles, let alone someone with a large child attached to their frontage via a complicated strap and sling thing. Anyhow, we sailed on and into our destination.

My father had sadly died by this time, having never met BB, and my mother was now elderly and did not drive. So there was no one to greet us at my home town when we got off the train in Barnstaple. We walked to the hotel, overnight bag in hand and BB happily clamped to my chest. I can feel his weight and his warmth now, zipped up in his red jungle-print padded outdoor onesie, his furrowed brow quizzing me. He gave me his cynical 'What the hell is going on?' look. I returned his puzzled gaze, and smiled ruefully, unsure myself.

We arrived at the hotel. I was out of puff and could have done with a large beverage, of the alcoholic variety, ideally, but the responsibility of lone parenting thwarted this particular desire. That and the gravity of going to court the following day, plus notes written two years hitherto to get acquainted with.

Arrangements had been made that my ex-manager would come to the hotel and hand me the relevant records ready for the following morning. I had to be prepared to answer any question relating to the case and the decisions I had made. We met in the hotel lobby and she handed over the notes. Great. Thank you. I was due at County Court at 10am the following morning.

I tried to make us at home in the room. I decided that it was a bit warm. It was an unseasonably hot May and the central heating was on at full blast. But the thermostat wouldn't budge. I wrestled with it. Swigging water like it was going out of fashion, I called room service to ask if someone else had the knack. A shiny waist-coated man arrived who was equally clueless. Could we possibly change rooms at all? We were going to roast if we stayed here.

Shiny waistcoat kindly showed us to another room at the rear of the hotel, with a view of the pub across a very narrow street. I could almost touch the pub if I leant out of the window, it was so close. Still, it was a decent temperature now and BB seemed to be calmer.

We unpacked again. I tried to get to grips with the blessed notes. Did I follow procedures? It was the first time that I had been called to court and I was utterly terrified. Read. Concentrate. Think. What is the judge likely to ask? I would likely have to explain my thinking and actions at the time of a critical safeguarding concern, which had eventually led to a legal intervention. Had we done the right thing? More to the point, had I done the right thing? It felt very much as though I had at the time, but we were two years on now so it was hard to remember, even with the luxury of records before me. And barristers can be tricky to deal with, maybe asking a leading question, which potentially gets us into an intellectual cul-de-sac.

Eight pm. The disco started in the pub a couple of feet away. At volume. No. Really? Yep. A bloody disco had just cranked up. Gloria Gaynor singing *I Will Survive* and Free singing *All Right Now*. No, we were certainly not all right now. Or later. It was questionable if I *was* going to survive. The music was relentless, as was BB's crying. How am I meant to concentrate? I called my sister who lived around the corner. She would help; she had offered earlier in the week. She wasn't in.

Needless to say, I was pretty desperate by now. My mother lived in a one-bed house and wouldn't be able to accommodate us. There was only one thing for it. I called Yvette. She was also a health visitor. We had, vaguely, kept in touch after I left the area – Christmas cards, the odd phone call – though we hadn't really meaningfully communicated for ages. But she was insightful and kind. She would also understand what I was going through professionally. Wouldn't she?

'Pack your bag. I'll be there in 10 minutes,' she said, as soon as I had explained the situation.

Oh, thank you, thank you, a million thank yous.

Yvette arrived, smiling, scooped us up, and whisked us up to her lovely warm and comfortable home that smelt of lasagne and Lenor. She ushered us into a freshly laundered bedroom. There was even a cot. Did I want dinner? Neil had just cooked.

We chatted about the proceedings for the following day. She soothed and reassured and all was well with the world. They were brilliant. Thank you so much. 'Be kind. For everyone you meet is fighting a hard battle.' It was and always has been so apt a saying, but particularly so that night.

Yvette took me to court and had offered to look after BB whilst I was captive there. It was a whirl of people, bodies, chatter.

'Where's Crystal?'

'Not here yet.'

Ah, there's Rose, social worker. 'Are you nervous?'

'Yep.'

'Oh, you've had a baby! That's amazing.'

'Actually, he's three months old and the milk ducts in my veiny boobs are leaking like overflowing rivulets as we speak. Not sure how long it'll be before I soak through the breast pads and blouse and then the jacket,' I thought, but didn't say. I envisaged the judge addressing a large puddle in the dock.

Crystal rocked up, took one look at all of us and legged it out of the courtroom. The case collapsed. All the expense, inconvenience, tears, frustration, mileage, train journeys, legal fees, crying baby, hotel room changes… Still, every cloud – not having to give evidence meant that I lived to dread it another day.

Yvette came to collect me, handing over BB, who had just wanted some water in my absence. I hugged her and thanked her so much for her help and generosity. We couldn't have done it without her. She deposited us at the train station and we clambered aboard, exhausted and relieved to be heading home. We pulled away, lolling and loping on the twisting, trundling train to the safety of our nest 200 miles away.

* * *

It was just before Christmas and a lovely midwife called to tell me that there was a new baby that I needed to take nappies and clothes for when I did the new birth visit on day 10-14. Enquiring as to why the family had no items for the baby, it transpired that, allegedly, the mother to the baby girl was a prostitute and her partner was her pimp. She had been captured on a hotel's CCTV 10 days post-delivery taking a 'client' back to the room, so it would seem that the couple were a bit too distracted to be getting to grips with the parenting thing.

I remember I was wearing a navy jumper and Black Watch tartan skirt, above the knee, but only just. I parked at some distance to the hotel but it was the closest I could get. I entered the hotel with my scales and bits and bobs for the baby; the main desk and manager's office was closed. I had the room number and found, after much wandering around, on the third floor, the appropriate room.

The short blonde girl concerned opened the door, let me in and we sat together on a blood-stained, soiled mattress with no sheets, blankets or quilt. Just two pillows, sans cases. There was a cot for baby, but no sheets again. It was pretty sparse. Very sparse, actually, and we discussed why there were no things for the baby. They were homeless and had no family. Their benefits hadn't come through. I opened the carrier bag with stuff for baby and she appeared happy to have more contributions.

Dad to baby (possibly, maybe) appeared and, like his girlfriend, was smiley and keen to engage, initially, making all the right noises. But it was still quite a puzzle to encounter this level of lack of preparation. We would need to contact social care to help with money, nappies, formula milk, etcetera, going forward. Oh no. They would be fine, thanks, was the reply. No need to involve social workers, they firmly emphasised.

There was a loud banging on the door and a sweaty looking red-haired freckled chap stood there, excitedly uttering, 'I've got a rock, I've got a rock.' Both men then disappeared into the en-suite bathroom for a good while. My antennae were telling me something was up, but this was 1991 and I still had lots to learn.

The mum and I talked about making up formula feeds, sterilising bottles, safe sleeping positions for baby in the cot, chasing up the benefits – could they use the hotel phone to do this? (Mobiles were not a thing then.) Was she bleeding very much at all? What was she going to do for contraception? She smiled at me and laughingly replied, 'I'll use condoms' – she thought my question was funny. She could charge more for sex without a condom, after all. I knew that much. I was beginning to wonder what was happening in the bathroom.

The chaps then appeared from the en-suite. Both were sweating profusely, eyes wide and pupils dilated. The atmosphere had changed. It felt menacing now. The questions were turned on me. Where did I live? Not locally. Was I married? That's not really appropriate. Do you have kids? Yes. How many? One. Oh. I thought you might have at least 12. Both laughed. They were looking directly at my legs. My skirt, just above the knee, now felt way too short. I needed to get out. The girl was laughing too, so no sisterly solidarity here. I was their 'sport'. They were still sweating, staring fixedly at me.

There are moments when you feel and know that your own safety is paramount. This was one of them. Something was brewing, and it wasn't going to end well. I made an excuse that I was late for another visit, picked up my scales and stated that I would see them at the child health clinic next week. I gave them a leaflet with the days, the times, the directions to the clinic, and the health visiting telephone number. And then I ran.

Legging it out the door and galloping down the stairs, I needed to get to my car, ASAP. As I swung past the main desk that had been closed on my arrival, I noticed it was now open and the hotel manager was in situ. I could hear footsteps on the stairs behind me. Heart racing, something told me – that inner voice – that I had to stop right there with the manager and take stock of what had just happened, and bat the breeze with him. Pretend I wasn't perturbed at all.

The hotel manager invited me to sit down and, at that point, the two men from whom I had fled passed the window, on their way out. I smiled at them. They stared at me but couldn't disguise their disappointment. The immediate realisation that I was protected and with the manager resulted in the rapid evaporation of their tepid smiles into fixed rictus grins. I absolutely felt that they had left their room with very bad intentions toward me and I will always be incredibly grateful that the manager was present as I left. Outside was a busy flyover with endless and incessant traffic, but no passing pedestrians. I would have been isolated and vulnerable had I gone out as they had anticipated.

Handle With Care

After an extended chat, I jogged tentatively to my car parked a good distance away, constantly checking behind and around me. I got in, locked the door, and effectively did an American-cop style handbrake turn to get the hell out of there and back to the office.

Chapter Six
Limehouse Health Visitor

In 1992, whilst still living in Hackney, I got a job as a health visitor in a GP practice in Limehouse to be closer to BB's childcare. It was an amazing time. I worked with a wonderful team of doctors, nurses and receptionists, including several Bangladeshi women who were invaluable as interpreters.

One of the GPs was David Widgery, a famous Trotskyite, radical and political activist in the East End with the Socialist Workers Party. He was the author of a book called *Some Lives – A GP's East End* (among other publications), which was one of the forerunners of the narrative style of medical memoirs. He was also the star of a documentary, *Limehouse Doctor*, being made at the surgery. There was a lot of being 'mic'd up' and people with furry boom microphones accompanying us out in our cars to visit families. It got to be incessant; we could only take the mic off if we went for a wee.

Dave had met Allan Ginsberg and had encountered the civil rights movement in the US, and had been heavily influenced by these events. There were other exploits, too, such as editing *Oz* magazine. A bit of an outsider, he had suffered polio as a child and walked with a distinctive limp. He was engaging, easy-going and humane – a delight to work with. Dave and the other GPs were unconventional, inclusive, funny and would have cared not one jot had I shared my Traveller/Gypsy roots with them. (I didn't, though. You just never knew if someone would take against it.) The surgery was a hub for the underdog, the marginalised, and totally committed to the multi-cultural.

We were getting used to the constant filming for the documentary, and then something shocking and bewildering happened. Dave died. Prematurely and unexpectedly. One of the other GPs came up to our office to share the news. We all shook our heads, stunned. 'But I only saw him couple of days ago…' The fierce, rebellious, heroic, anti-capitalist, decent and sweet colleague was gone.

The documentary went ahead in tribute to him. There was a packed memorial at the Hackney Empire to which the surgery staff were invited – there was a load of musicians, politicos and polemicists paying tribute to celebrate his life. Paul Foot, nephew of Michael Foot and political campaigner and journalist, was amongst them.

We regrouped and carried on, though now very much on the media's radar, whenever they wanted an opinion on the organisation of healthcare, or something similar. One morning, I found myself being advised there was a team from Carlton TV coming to do a piece on poverty and the link to low uptake of immunisations. I duly obliged and took the journalist, producer, sound and a few others on a walkabout. There was a discussion about how grinding poverty permeates your everything. Your thoughts. Your wellbeing. Your choices – or lack of them. And how when it comes to getting babies and children immunised, it wasn't always at the top of the agenda for those eking out a living and worrying about where the next pay cheque was coming from. Or possibly transport issues simply inhibited getting to the clinic for an appointment.

Someone else recorded it for us, as we had elected not to have a TV at home at that point. I still have it on video somewhere.

There was always an excuse to cook at this surgery, especially if there was a birthday or a GP trainee had completed their rotation and was saying goodbye – we would all bring in a dish to share at lunchtime or occasionally jam ourselves into several cars for a trip to the culinary delights of vibrant Brick Lane. The curry capital of London. This area was Spitalfields, but was latterly christened Bangla Town. Our celebratory activities were set against the backdrop of the call to prayer coming from the nearby mosques and the jostle and thrum of a vibrant neighbourhood with an amazing history.

In 1860, a treaty with France enabled the import of cheaper French silks. The Huguenots were famously associated with the silk industry – they arrived into this part of London with little other than their skills, and soon Irish weavers came to take up the new silk trade, having suffered the decline of the Irish linen industry. New trades such as furniture making and boot making then came to the area. There were robbers and prostitutes and slums, Jack the Ripper and the Whitechapel murders; there were riots with the decline of the silk industry, then more riots on Cable Street when the fascist Black-shirts, at the behest of Oswald Moseley, marched and clashed with the police and the Jewish community. In the late 20th century, the Jewish presence diminished and gave way to the Bangladeshi community, who also worked in the textile trade and who remain there to this day as one of the largest Bangladeshi communities in Europe.

The history of Limehouse, where the surgery I worked from was based, is equally fascinating. The earliest reference dates back to 1356, when the district was known as 'Les Lymhostes' due to its connections with the pottery industries. It was also the perfect landing spot for boats and ships, and the first wharf was constructed in 1348 as it became a leading centre for world trade for London. Sir Francis Drake set off for one of his voyages from Limehouse Wharf. Samuel Pepys wrote a short piece about a visit to a porcelain factory, and one of the pubs, The Grapes, was a favourite drinking den of Charles Dickens. In more recent times, Sir Ian McKellan purchased the pub, and his staff from his time as Gandalf is propped up behind the bar. It's always been a magnet for immigrants from around the globe.

Limehouse was London's original Chinatown, and there was still a Chinese community there as well as a large Bangladeshi community. When we visited the local Muslim families in Limehouse, they would sit you down with a small table to your side, and Bangladeshi treats – curries, samosas, rice, the whole kit and caboodle – would be placed adjacent to you. So generous and kind. It was impossible to diet in this line of work.

There was still a preponderance of white working-class families in the area, too, some who were lucky enough to have their family nearby. Then there were the 'uppers' who were beginning to move in and gentrify the area, though still, at this time, living amongst the West Indian families, the Vietnamese and Chinese. The pie and mash shop was next to the Indonesian takeaway, next to the fried chicken shop, and all a stone's throw from Canary Wharf and the car parks saturated with luxury, high-end cars. What a mix!

* * *

I was in the early stages of a second pregnancy and we had booked a holiday back in the West Country. The MS *Oldenburg*, Lundy's historic ferry, transported us from Ilfracombe to Lundy Island. It was just the sanctuary we needed, away from the pressure of London life. The isolated wilderness of the half-mile-wide, three-mile-long island was spectacular.

We hired a cottage, Stoneycroft, next to The Old Light, Beacon Hill. There was a pub – the Marisco Tavern – a shop, and a church that was the hub of the daily nature sightings: a chalk board would be displayed outside if basking sharks or puffins or Manx shearwaters had been spotted. That was it in terms of 'first world' provisions. Other than the sea and the birds, the only noise you might hear would be the squealing of children. There were wild Lundy ponies which chased us if we were carrying bread on our way to feed the 'sucky' fish (koi carp) in a nearby pond. There weren't any TVs in the holiday properties. The electricity went off at midnight, so after enjoying refreshments at the pub and wending your way home, you were dependent upon your torch, and the stars, of course. But we were generally back well before dark, tucked up, having spent the day reading, flying kites, having a cream tea in the front garden and playing board games amidst the rarefied tranquillity.

The morning would involve a cooked breakfast and the writing of postcards – or illustrating of them, in BB's case. He drew pictures of sharks and seals and starfish for friends and family. This would be followed by a walk down to the bay for a swim, which took us past the pub, which was also the post office, so we could post our cards.

We often sat watching the seals. They were bottling in that upright way that they do. There was a gaggle of goings on; nosing and glossy blinking and wet whiskering. Their guttural, maternal and ancient cries resonated around the island in late August. I was full of pregnancy hormones, although it was still early days.

The island warden had organised a snorkelling session one afternoon, so with J. looking after BB, I selected a fitting dry suit, met with the happy gathering of fellow snorkelers and, after discussing the rules and regs, we buddied up, learnt the signs to make for 'I'm OK', 'I want to go back', 'Let's go', and then tally-ho, we dived in.

Spluttering through the pipe but gathering myself and gaining in confidence, ducking and gasping, I surveyed the astonishing view below. There was a carnival of colour and a choreographed, graceful dance of sea creatures: a world of turquoise, fleshy starfish and striped yellows, pinks and bright blues flashing, scuttling and darting in and out of the rocky outcrops, sand and seaweeds, for all the world like a carefully prepared silent and dazzling Pixar movie.

One of the seals was close by and, although the others deserted her, she hung on. She was beautiful in that way that nature up close often is. She seemed reluctant to leave, was standing by, or so it felt, her proximity mesmerising.

After what seemed an age of swimming close to us, she dived off and started to wail. I suddenly felt very cold and signalled to my buddy that I wished to return to the rocks that we had set out from. I had an urgent need to pee.

I clambered back to the rocky shoreline and, crouching behind a series of rocks, I pulled down my dry-suit. I was peeing pink. Slightly disbelieving, I double checked. Nope, it was definitely pink. Had I cut myself on the rocks getting out? Going in? Where was I bleeding from? Of course, it was the only kind of bleeding, the dreaded bleeding – the one that leaves you reeling and confused. I was losing my baby and I'm sure the seal had sensed it, hovering and concerned.

It was painless (another miscarriage some time later informed me that not all miscarriages were so), but a lift back to the top of the island in the warden's Land Rover was gratefully accepted. On returning to our cottage, next to the lighthouse, I realised that perhaps I hadn't miscarried completely.

What if I haven't? I fretted. With 'retained products', I really would be in trouble. The warden dropped by later that day, suggesting that the local helicopter fly me off the island to the nearest hospital. I was OK. Not in pain but still bleeding: silent, painless bleeding. BB was quiet and contemplative. J. was fussing over me and forlorn. We decided that I didn't need a helicopter and sailed off the island several days later, leaving my mermaid foetus with the calling and watchful seal who had hung back from the others.

I was quite stressed out at this point and felt that the miscarriage was a result of this. Not only was I working full time, but I had started a part-time master's in health policy, planning and financing at the LSE in collaboration with the London School of Hygiene. I was attending on a 'day release' basis and it ran for two years.

I was slightly amazed at being there and I enjoyed every second, trotting up to Holborn tube to join the others who were destined for organising healthcare overseas. I was happy in the knowledge that overseas wasn't for me. I was just glad to be there and was beginning to think that a move into healthcare management − into a role organising and directing teams and determining how the service was delivered − might be a possibility.

The course was designed to develop critical analysis of issues relating to health, planning and financing in order to develop health policy. We studied organisational management, health economics – I even think I understood cost benefit analysis at one point! We made presentations to our tutor, Professor Le Grand. We examined global and national policies and had to write fairly complex reports and presentations.

There were lots of animated debates between us – in our group there were right-wing Americans, a social worker from Norway, a Spanish healthcare policy maker and more than a smattering from Africa getting ready to return to apply their knowledge and skills to the setting up of healthcare teams across their continent to operate in disaster zones and places stricken by famine and war.

It was a busy old time, what with both J. and me working full time, doing the master's, looking after one lively four-year-old and two properties – both in negative equity – our home in Hackney and the house in Barnstaple, which was now often empty but unsaleable due to an ongoing slow-down in the property market.

* * *

Halloween 1995 and I am bleeding again, this time in the Hackney branch of Marks and Sparks, if you please. Weirdly witchy and pagan. BB and I are choosing supper, when an intense pain heralds a heavy, heavy bleed and then the contractions kick in. The miscarriage on Lundy was totally painless, but this is the polar opposite. BB looks, understandably, a tad scared. I wonder how I can get to hospital and look after him, what with J. at work and both sets of extended family over 200 miles away.

I approach an assistant, she gathers us up and sits us down at the end of the checkouts, calmly informing me that she will call the ambulance. Spotting my neighbour, I hear a fanfare in my head. Yes! Somebody who can help us – thank you God and all my lucky stars. Heather is Home Counties and a nurse. Solid, approachable, kind. I have known her for some years. She can take BB home and he will be safe and protected from this bloody mess, of that I can be sure. They exit stage left, holding hands as she sweetly soothes him.

Then I start to howl. Loudly. The contractions are bloody painful and customers, mainly large elderly women, rubber neck as they walk slowly past with their bulky carrier bags and puzzled faces. I don't really remember the journey in the ambulance, nor do I recall how J. got to be at the Homerton when I arrived at A&E, but he was, and I was glad.

We were parked in a side room and a kind, fair-haired doctor swished in from behind a curtain in a haze of weary but resolute efficiency. She told me that, with such a colossal blood loss, it was highly likely that the eight-week foetus was lost. She would scan me. The cold, slimy gel was squirted over my abdomen and the ultrasound scooched around the slippery skin looking for a baby that wouldn't be there.

There was a bright light flashing, rhythmically and sure. 'Well, I'll be… Someone is still in there,' the medic announced with raised eyebrows.

'It is possible, if bleeding in the early weeks, to have originally had a twin pregnancy and to have lost one. It certainly looks that way. Hard to diagnose but more likely than you'd think,' she explained.

But my baby was clinging on. Yay! My witchy girl. Snug and cosy. I felt she was smiling to herself, in a 'I'm staying right here' kind of way. Dug into the warm, half-lit, blood-whooshed uterus, which was home for now. I imagined her in a tiny, flimsy Halloween costume with a slashed hem, gauze wings and pointy hat, guzzling toffee apples and giggling like a Buddha.

Seven months later, on a sweltering midsummer morning, she was gently placed on my chest: my faerie witch daughter, wearing the jagged hem of the cawl and membranes, smelling of sea salty amniotic fluid, with a proper Elvis style shock of hair. She's 'been before', they said. She knew how to breast-feed from the off and, in between the sleeping and the feeding, she would murmur and wriggle. Gorgeous Girl. GG, as she will be referred to henceforth.

My beautiful, feisty, wilful daughter, GG, with her glossy chestnut mane like a Herbal Essences ad and her coltish legs up to her armpits. In the intervening 24 years she, of course, has been delightful – festival-going, waitressing, hard-working, fashion store supervisor, fierce defender of justice. Her early months were particularly stressful, however. Having two children and working in Tower Hamlets was not without its challenges.

Though there were some advantages of our London life. BB was a pupil at a Bangladeshi school and was enjoying this immensely. He had numerous friends and was always being invited somewhere for tea. Some days he would return home with a Mendi hand, a henna temporary tattoo to celebrate Eid, and when he attended nursery in Stepney, there was a 'Mother' Christmas one year to pass out the presents. Benjamin Zephaniah fabulously attended the school to read his poetry to the children. We were lucky to have access to such inspiring schools and BB was having a great time.

* * *

I was back at work after having GG. However, actually getting to work was becoming a problem, as my car was being clamped regularly when I was in the process of dropping GG with her child minder. They went through a phase of waiting for me each morning. Bloody hell. I had to run up the stairwell to Karen;

she would keep look out, shouting, 'They're coming! they're coming!' I would leg it down the stairs after quickly kissing GG's head. Sometimes I beat the clampers – but not today.

Though I pleaded with him, he continued with his chain and immobiliser (but couldn't look me in the eye) and issued me with the sticky ticket. I then had to wait for someone to come and unclamp me again, but only if I coughed up the required £60 via debit or credit card. All before the day's work. I once got clamped when delivering £20 (own money again – I'm not *really* a soft touch) to a mother with an empty purse whose husband was going into hospital that day. Buggerations. Give a girl a break!

I went through the now familiar process to get unclamped and finally headed off to work, where I experienced one of the most hair-raising of professional experiences, ever. I was undertaking a new birth visit to Jean and her new baby Chloe, who were living in a homeless shelter. There was always a sense of underlying bedlam and menace there. I was never entirely sure who or what I was going to encounter. You can sometimes smell the impending chaos looming. And the booze.

This particular morning, after discovering that Jean was making feeds with a famous brand of sparkling H_2O (a complete no-no due to sodium and nitrite content), there was an almighty screaming. It was getting closer and louder until a short, plump woman came galloping into the flat, threw herself into the vacant chair next to me, hands over her mouth, continuing to scream but all the while staring at me. Why is she yelling at full throttle? And why is she looking at me?

I was just about to ask when in strode a huge – and I mean huge – bloke holding a very long knife. Now, I am no expert in knives, so when asked later by the policeman whether it was a bread knife or a machete, I had no idea, save to say it had a bloody long blade. And he was now holding it up in the air.

'Get up!' was the instruction. 'Get up, you fucking bitch.'

Sorry, but was he talking to the screaming woman? Or me? Jean? All of us? In that second of trying to make sense of what was happening, nothing made sense at all. He was standing at the entrance to the flat. Fuck. He's going to kill us. That's it then. Time is up.

No, we are getting out! In that moment, I knew I had to try.

There was a certain intense, breathless swirling of thoughts and emotions and then something resembling a decision came out. I don't know where I summoned the notion, but in my most authoritative voice, I stood and loudly proclaimed, 'Right Jean, I think we're leaving now. Bring Chloe.'

Her anxious frown glared at me as if to say, you are quite mad, aren't you? She cautiously did as I asked and lifted her out of the Moses basket, baby blankets flapping around her tiny frame. I took her keys which were on the coffee table, picked up my cumbersome weighing scales and, throwing them as nonchalantly as I could over my shoulder, we edged toward him. I can feel his proximity now. His huge frame blocking the doorway. Christ, he's enormous.

As I faux confidently got level with him he asked, 'You OK, lady?' in a surprisingly soothing manner.

In that moment, I believed, or hoped, he wasn't going to harm us. His tone was not one of a mass murderer, was it? 'Yes, fine thanks,' was my reply.

Fuck. My throat was hot and dry and it was a miracle that anything came out at all. Fine? What sort of a lame response was that? Maybe he was lulling us into thinking that he wasn't about to maniacally strike, but simply wrong-footing us?

I ushered Jean out first, then turned to screaming woman and gestured to the door, 'Are you coming?' She sat rooted to the chair and shook her head. Jean, holding her bundle of Chloe, and me with my scales over my shoulder, ran hell for leather down the stairs, checking all the while to assess if huge bloke had done a volte-face and was pursuing us.

We ran out into the street, me ungainly galloping ahead with a flailing black bag of scales handicapping my jog, and Jean not far behind with her precious bundle, all blankets flying, down the busy road full of traffic and into the surgery which, thankfully, was close by. After catching our breath, we called the police, who reluctantly visited the surgery later that day to say that they had investigated our incident but the woman at the shelter said that nothing had happened, had declined to press charges, and so it probably wasn't worth their while filling in paperwork, if that was all the same to me.

I telephoned my line manager, thinking, well, this was a significant event, before we even thought of significant events as a proper thing – like they are now. She asked if I was frightened. 'Yes, of course!' I replied. OK. Nothing else to say. I don't even think she asked if I had to go back to said family and property. Which I did. I'm not really sure that some of our managers who sit in their offices, miles away from the real world, actually get the dangers that we face out there. Anyhow, another eventful day in our inner cities.

The moral of this tale of course is, do not, under any circumstances, make your baby's bottles of formula milk with Perrier. Ever. It could lead to all sorts of chaos. And police intervention.

After all the shenanigans of that particular visit, I had to ensure that this baby was safe in an ongoing sense. Later that week, I trotted along to the shelter with the obligatory weighing scales. On approaching the shared flat, I could see that the front door was wide open. I tentatively entered, calling Jean's name. No answer. I cautiously entered.

'Hello? Helloooo?' No response. Just echo. No one in the living area or kitchen. Lots of empties duly noted. Hmmm.

I tentatively poked my head around Jean's bedroom door and saw baby Chloe in a crib with a lighted candle still burning in a saucer on a bedside cabinet. She was asleep and seemingly fine, but alone. I blew the candle out. Nowadays we have a policy that if we find a child under five alone, we call the police, but this was the mid-90s. There was no policy because it was fairly uncommon. Plus there weren't any work mobiles and Jean didn't have a landline anyway.

I sat in the doorway on the floor with my head in my hands. Footsteps were coming up the stairs. 'This will be her,' I thought. I watched as a WPC turned the final corner of the stairwell and swung into view.

'Hello,' she said suspiciously, looking at me looking at her equally confused. 'I've popped round as there was some disturbance here last night, a domestic. Parents had been drinking heavily. Is everything OK?'

No, it most definitely was not. 'This baby, five weeks old, is on her own and had a burning candle next to her,'

I explained. I'd never been so glad to see help (although we could have done with her on the occasion of bloke with knife as well, but hey, I'll take any assistance I can get).

I showed her into the bedroom where Chloe lay in her crib, blissfully unaware of the gravity of the situation. Or was she? Maybe it had been a night of disruptions and disturbances for her, too. When did she last feed? Had she only just got to sleep herself? What if she was injured? We gave her a superficial once-over; she appeared uninjured but it was clear that she was very much in danger, having been abandoned with only a lighted candle for company.

The WPC said that she was going to issue an EPO (an emergency protection order, nowadays entitled a police protection order, PPO), which allows the police to remove a child to a place of safety.

With that, Jean appeared. Completely pissed. It was 10.30am. She was naked save for a small multi-coloured crocheted blanket and was ridiculously delighted to see us.

'Ah, Rachael! Would you like to fuck?'

'Er… Sorry? Erm… no thanks, if it's all the same to you, it's a bit early and I'm a bit busy – we're going to take your baby to hospital for safety. Just until you sober up.'

'Ah,' she said, 'you always were a bit stuck up.'

I chuckled at that one. Yep, royalty, me.

* * *

In Tower Hamlets, we worked with Muslim families alongside Sylheti-speaking interpreters – you can get by a bit with a few gestures and smiles, but to find out what's really going on you need an interpreter if your client doesn't speak English. There was a brilliant service called Language Line, where if you needed an interpreter for any language you could just phone and request Mandarin, Cantonese, Farsi, Polish… any language at all. It made the job so much easier as you could explain to the interpreter what you needed to glean and then pass the phone to your client, who would have the required conversation with the person at other end and then hand the phone back to you, so you could ascertain what the situation was. The Bangladeshi community included some of the poorest in the area.

Each Christmas, there was an event held by Capital Radio, called 'Help a Capital Child at Christmas', whereby generous folk would contribute either money or children's toys. Charities and professionals such as health visitors and social workers would head up to Euston Road to pick up the donations, hoping to catch a glimpse of Chris Tarrant, who hosted the station's flagship Breakfast Show for what seemed like decades. The jingle is still locked in to my brain: 'Oooh you send me – Tarrant on the radio.'

My colleagues and I would wrestle several large bags to the car, head back to our office in Limehouse and plonk everything on the floor until we got time to sort the mound of brand new toys into probable gender suitability (don't hate me – blame the mid-90s), wrap them and apply a tag that denoted the suggested age range. They would then be delivered to our families closer to the festivities.

The whole point of it was to help those who were struggling to provide for their families seamlessly. If you haven't ever gone without then it may appear a tad patronising, but believe me, when you really are in need, all help is so very gratefully received. The presents were also distributed regardless of religion or culture. It was about need, after all.

At this time, I was running a weekly baby clinic – a staple feature of health visiting –from a deeply uninspiring room in a block of neglected flats, called John Scurr House. (I should point out this block was happily revamped at some point later in the decade.) I decided I would use the same space to start a healthy eating group for the resident families. Each week, I would organise a TV with a video about healthy eating to share the information for the prevention of diabetes, which is prevalent in the Bangladeshi community. We covered a different topic every time, and each week the same families would diligently attend and then wait patiently at the end to ask about housing.

It struck me as overwhelming that the families' health and life chances were defined by the misfortune of living in this block. There were mattresses abandoned on stairwells, needles and syringes too. It was grim. And perilously close to the trains which would thunder by hellishly. I thought that I should do something about it.

My colleagues and I decided to attend Parliament to lobby the shadow housing minister to see what could be done. We approached the Palace of Westminster. The policemen on the door vetted us and allowed us in. A 'ticket' was sent round to see if said minister was in the house. He was. A research assistant greeted us and asked about the reason for our visit. We explained that our work in Tower Hamlets was hampered by the astonishing lack of habitable and affordable housing. It was either luxury gated stuff or the John Scurr House variety.

He listened patiently and then started to veer off topic. Slightly puzzlingly, the fighting in East Timor was his favourite topic of conversation.

I was slightly bemused by his patter as it was clear that we were not in a position to influence anything in East Timor, but we could possibly do something about housing in our own country. Couldn't we?

So a housing clinic was actually set up – with a group of solicitors on the Mile End Road. I think there was some consternation surrounding the invitation of solicitors onto NHS premises – our health centre, which is where it would be run on a weekly basis.

Before its inception, I met with the team of legal professionals in the Blind Beggar pub (made famous by the Kray twins) and we had a brief chat about the need for the housing clinic. It was desperately needed. There were cockroaches, rats, overcrowding, disrepair and enough damp and mould to trigger an immediate asthma attack – before the estate was eventually redeveloped.

* * *

Around about this time, London life really began to take its toll. I vividly remember going to pick up the children from Karen's, the child minder who looked after GG and would also collect BB from school.

She and her family lived in a high-rise block in Tower Hamlets. It was Bonfire Night. A cold wind whipped around the buildings' sharp concrete edges and took my breath away. It was dark, I was tired and pulling my coat around me. I was looking forward to picking up the kids to go home, cook supper and continue with our recently acquired reading scheme for BB. (Most professionals, at that time, taught their offspring to read at home using a phonics method – there was a well-trodden path of taking two weeks off work to do so.)

I leaned into the buzzer on the intercom only to puzzle over a vaguely familiar whistling sound, then bang! A firework landed at my feet, having been thrown from nowhere and for no apparent reason. Fucksakes!

I squealed and looked around for some thoughtless twat that might have been responsible. No one around. It must have been thrown from one of the high-rise windows. What if I had been hit? What if the children had been with me? Bursting into tears, I tried to compose myself for BB, GG and Karen. Snotty, red-eyed and dishevelled, I collected both children, jogging a bit quicker than usual to get back to the safety of the car.

I don't know why, but this particular incident felt like the catalyst for some hard decision-making that we had been avoiding. We had wanted to move back to the West Country, but still hadn't got round to it. I felt like I was the worst parent, the worst health visitor – and now this bloody firework! Everything at that moment felt wrong. I yearned for the West Country. Somewhere that we could call home. It just felt that Hackney, for us, right then, was the wrong place for the children to be in terms of life chances.

Chapter Seven
Goodbye, London

We moved to Dorset on the 1st May 1997. Blair was duly elected as things 'could only get better'. Couldn't they? We followed our removal truck, whizzing down the M3 to our new abode. We had decided that we wanted BB and GG to be as free range as possible; to have unfettered access to the sea and all things green with big, open skies and horizons. J. had secured a new position there in IT project management and we were giddy with optimism.

I took a year off, to settle us all into our new life. There was much walking to school for BB, a nearby trout farm for purchasing something for supper, and the neighbouring fields beckoned frequently. There was the baking of biscuits and sponges for the school fairs, trips to the seaside, fishing for tiddlers in a nearby stream for BB, while GG looked on, ensconced in a tartan buggy. We had BB's whole class in our kitchen dancing to the Spice Girls at one point, and we happily joined a throng of misfits and eccentrics of all ages at a 'coffee group' in the local church hall, where country and western was played on an old-fashioned turntable. It was a mish-mash of playgroup for toddlers, café, jumble sale and tea dance for the elderly. Quite brilliant, actually. A dynamic lady in the village had started it.

It was a shock in some ways to be in the countryside – a good one in almost every way, for the greenery and fresh air and tranquillity, but one of the downsides that we hadn't considered was that you couldn't eat French cuisine at 5pm on a Sunday afternoon as you might in London! We were used to being able to get world foods – and at any time – back in the smoke, but everything here was closed pretty much from Sunday lunchtime.

The children were used to being taken out for meals. BB had developed a taste for Thai and Indian food; even GG, who was 10 months when we moved, was accustomed to having a pureed or finger-food portion of whatever we were eating – be it a Turkish pide, which is a bit like a pizza, or a making a mess with the Guajarati thali, a selection of samosas, roti, dal, that sort of scrumptiousness.

One of the first things that BB uttered when we moved was, 'Where are all the brown people, Mummy?' He was used to being one of only a handful of white children at his Bangladeshi school. I think we swapped multicultural, exuberant and sociable, spontaneous living for a quieter, more subdued, grown-up lifestyle. J. and I pined, a little, for the capital, but the wistfulness gave way to the new routines of picnic suppers on the beach at Lulworth Cove and masses of outdoorsy stuff for BB and GG when she was big enough to join in.

Eventually I joined the 'bank' of health visitors, working part time, after unsuccessfully applying for a vacant post in a neighbouring village – I wasn't even shortlisted! Blooming cheek! They probably thought I was a 'snooty' London type, but I cunningly manoeuvred myself into covering a few sessions at that very surgery and, after a second application, it was clear that I had worn them down and they gave in! I was appointed and remained there, happily, for almost 10 years.

There were visits to those in the armed services and their families where the wives and children would dwell largely without their spouses for great chunks of their lives. I would have to check into the security on base and have the scanner applied to the car to check for bombs, or whatever it is they check for. There were farmers, fishermen, lawyers, artists, authors, divers, soldiers, teachers, bankers, builders, thatchers, scientists, doctors –you name it. All kinds of folk of all persuasions and colours and creeds and their families. Yes, even in sleepy Dorset.

It was pretty strange though, in a health visiting sense, as a lot of the problems that I encountered in various Dorset villages when I returned to work seemed to be of an urban nature but in a rural setting: drugs, domestic abuse, poverty – although here in the sticks it could be hidden behind a chocolate-box exterior.

Some of the pretty thatched cottages in a bucolic setting were especially prone to such a juxtaposition and it was sometimes hard to get others, like social care, to take it seriously when they didn't, or couldn't, witness what we saw first-hand (a perennial problem in our line of work). I think it's a frustration that we all share, that if there's squalor but without much of a safeguarding concern (although the two sometimes are linked), no one else will see what we see.

For example, perhaps the children aren't in any immediate danger, but they are playing on filthy carpets and grime-encrusted sparse furniture, and both children and adults are in grubby PJs all day long because there's nothing to go out for and they can't afford new clothes anyway.

We file our reports and send emails requesting help, but sometimes those receiving them just cannot grasp the impact that the stench of decay and paucity of options, joy and aspiration has on one's soul. Those at the end of a phone-call or a recipient of a zesty email – perhaps the housing association or the local MP – will privately think to themselves, 'Oh god, not her again,' but until they get to witness the truth, up close and personal, the wide-reaching impact of this sort of poverty on a family is hard for them to understand.

Oh, and the dentistry! Or rather, lack of it! It is, of course, a national scandal that dental surgery is, largely, a mysterious menu of varying and complex charges which inhibit patients from attending in the first place – everything is a bit opaque until, post-treatment, and incapable of coherent speech, you are flamboyantly presented with the eye-watering bill in front of an entire gawping waiting room, who witness the infuriated cries of, 'How much?' Or, more likely, 'Aaah buch?' in a snivelling drool. For goodness' sake, can't somebody in government overhaul that particular conundrum?

I contacted someone from a housing association regarding a family living in squalor in a pretty, much sought-after village, in one of their properties. The bloke was reluctant to come out, even though it was his job to offer support to tenants. I threatened to contact his CEO if he didn't and suddenly he was falling over himself to join me. A skip was organised to enable the family to chuck out their old and broken furniture (which was most of it), tenancy support was put in place which enabled various DIY projects to be addressed, and I managed to apply for a slew of new furniture from a very generous charity. So at least the family could make a new start and were given the space and opportunity to rethink and view things through a different prism.

Don't get me wrong, I'm all for families taking responsibility for themselves, but there's a world of difference between those who *refuse t*o and those who *cannot* because of mental health struggles or similar – or they just can't access any of the resources they need to sort themselves out. In this situation, they often just can't see beyond the whirl of chaos that they inhabit. Health visitors see this day in and day out; it is our own particular speciality and someone at a government level should be utilising us with greater effect to inform and shape health and social policy decisions and direction.

An encampment of New Age Travellers had recently moved into the area and a family with a new baby were discovered living on a bus, complete with wood-burner. Mum was of Traveller stock but had elected to join this particular merry band, who were more her age and with similar inclinations for festivals and traveller gatherings. Her baby girl was called Iris, named after the messenger to the Gods, on account of her being conceived in a telephone box near some ley lines.

I was delighted to be her health visitor, though there were several large and angry dogs on chains that had to be negotiated. (I was used to angry dogs by now. Hazard of the job.)

But the bus was very homely and I was made welcome with the offer of tea, which I eagerly accepted. Even one of the dogs joined us and sniffed me with an amiable disposition. It was next stop Glasto for the Travellers.

I was the only HV at the practice, though I was ably supported by a nursery nurse and admin lady. It meant that all the child protection decisions and report-writing was my responsibility alone. We had computers at this point but our records were still paper.

The admin assistant, nursery nurse and I all shared an office the size of a cupboard with about five district nurses who called the office home at any given time. Thankfully, we weren't in there all at once, but it was quite a jam when even a third of us turned up, and somewhat impossible to contemplate important child protection situations whilst phones trilled and lots of 'goss' about who did what to whom at the weekend was exchanged. I often used to write my reports at home due to the racket.

However, it was funny, supportive, wise, very maternal – even if it was also infuriating on occasions, with no peace or quiet, and too bloody nosy! We all knew a great deal about each other's work and problems, family or otherwise, but it was always a kind and sociable place to be. People would look after each other's dogs when they were going on holiday and cakes were brought in for general consumption. If the majority were on a diet (when weren't we?) one thoughtful GP would bring in a huge basket of strawberries sold from various lay-bys in Purbeck, locally grown and having travelled less than a mile.

One summer, a surgery game of rounders was organised on the village recreation ground. All were invited: partners, children and friends. We brought a picnic each and, amazingly, a cast filming *The Mayor of Casterbridge* at a nearby derelict watermill joined us for a while – they were staying close by and were quite taken with what the villagers got up to.

Sometimes, after a difficult day, we would have to get out after work. We'd head down to Lulworth Cove with our cozzies on under our clothes (or uniforms) and park in a secret spot that only the locals were aware of.

On one occasion, a snooty lady challenged us as we spilled out of my colleague's people carrier: 'Excuse me, this car park is for local people!' (Shades of *League of Gentlemen* there.)

'Yes,' my colleague retorted in her broad Yorkshire accent, 'We *are* law-kul.'

Snotty woman glared and sniffily went on her way. We thronged down to the shingle beach, left our goods and chattels at the shoreline and Laura, the lovely lead district nurse, plunged in first. Yikes, it was bloody freezing, of course!

After the initial shock one quickly acclimatises and it was indeed delicious and exhilarating. We squealed as the seaweed brushed against our legs, pretending we weren't scared, but secretly fearing it might be a fish or a shark. Then home with refreshing vim and vigour. It was the perfect antidote to work stress and we didn't do it nearly enough.

We were temporarily displaced into Portakabins while a new surgery was built. My office was in one; the district nurses were in an adjoining one. Occasionally I would take our border collie, Meg, with me to the makeshift office. The suggestion, 'Shall we go to work?' would send her excitedly jumping into the car. At work, she would tuck herself under the desk, quiet as a mouse, even when the phone trilled (although when the phone rang at home, it would send her barmy), looking very proud indeed.

However, she did have a penchant for barking at men in luminous jackets, so a spell of builders put a stop to her 'associate HV' position. There was also one incident when she escaped from 'her office' and ran up the lane while I rather lamely called after her. It occurred to me that she might prefer to be chasing me – collies are herding dogs, after all – so I reversed direction and began running away. *Quelle surprise*, she shot past me like a torpedo and laid down at my feet. Job done.

* * *

Health visitors have to have decent waterproofing as standard, really, due to being out and about in all weathers. I have spent too many winters in short, thin, hopeless jackets and you end up not only looking a mess – as though you can't look after yourself, let alone advise your clients – but you also drip unwelcome weather into your clients' homes.

So, faced with another Dorset winter, I purchased a brand new, crazily expensive, full-length brown waxed mackintosh. However, after its first excursion, it was pretty much ruined, and stank of weed for years to come. Dogs would sniff me intently, other folk would examine me quizzically on getting too close, and even my own children would tease me with, 'Mum likes a spliff, don't you Ma?'

(I really don't. I smoked one once when in my twenties after consuming a rather large quantity of gin and suffered something, unbeknownst to me at the time, called 'the whiteys'. I vomited continually, curled around a lavatory for most of a New Year's Eve party. Never touched cannabis ever again. Gin yes. Obligatory some days.)

The damage to my mac was caused when I decided to call on the Smith family, late one morning. On walking up the path, I was hit with the combination of Elvis belting out *Jailhouse Rock*, a male shouting incoherently, and the pungent aroma of cannabis.

Carrie opened the door and practically dragged me in by my new lapels. 'I'm glad you're here, he's driving me mad, sit down.' I did as I was told.

Gary shouted from the kitchen to Carrie, 'I love you, Caz. Come here, I'm reading our horoscopes.' He was sobbing like a baby, Elvis continued very loudly and three children under five were wailing in grubby baby grows and eating crap off the floor.

It's a feat of some nimbleness, I think, that I can listen to fraught mum and ask appropriate questions whilst simultaneously scanning a room, preventing toddlers from consuming a sticky Opal Fruit covered in dog hair (not compatible with a six-month-old at all) and retrieving a discarded strip of aspirin from the floor. There was also a child crawling enthusiastically toward a dog turd. Carrie scooped it after a little prompting. Usually a bit of pointed staring at it does the trick.

Gary had depression – and amongst other things, took his antidepressants erratically, drank more often than not, missed his mental health appointments, ran around in a beat-up Nissan despite never having taken a test, and caused mayhem generally. He had, of course, had a dysfunctional upbringing. Some days he would take off and be found sleeping at the local bus station. Today, he was home and clearly high.

Lordy, I could understand Carrie's frustration and why she was considering leaving him. The rent was in arrears, Gary would spend any money they had on substances, they had no food and he would return with all sorts of crazy bits of furniture picked up from the tip. In situ today in the considerably overcrowded living room was a set of grubby garden furniture complete with raised parasol (I was sitting under it).

Elvis continued with *You Ain't Nothing But a Hound Dog*; Gary continued with his spliff, shouting incomprehensibly in the kitchen, and Carrie poured out her woes, tired of dealing with the madness and with little family support. What could I do? They needed social services' intervention as the family were clearly not coping, but I knew any mention of social workers was going to get me kicked out. Both Gary and Carrie's mental health were clearly deteriorating along with the home situation; chaos and unsafe conditions reigned for these children. The youngest two of the three were losing weight due to lack of cash and they were unstimulated and unsupervised. There was nothing else for it; I had to be transparent.

There was much gnashing of teeth and cries of, 'They'll take the kids away.'

'No, they won't, but we can put in place a family support worker, someone who works with families to help with budgeting, parenting, housework, things like that, to help with the structuring of your day. They'll assist with budgeting which will, in turn, address the rent arrears. We could get a nursery placement for your three-year-old. We could get dedicated help with Gary's mental health. There are all sorts of ways that a social worker and a family support worker could help.'

Social care, thankfully, accepted my referral. But the next morning, I discovered that neighbours had called the police following an altercation the night before, so social workers became involved anyway. Carrie took off with the children to a family nearby; Gary was found in the garden asleep, surrounded by several cans of Special Brew and an array of other substance paraphernalia. Elvis had indeed left the building.

Two days after this, I discovered my car had a derogatory word keyed on the driver's side door. Whilst not being 100 per cent sure of its author, I suspected it was an unequivocal indictment in terms of how I was regarded in said family's esteem. Until I could afford a re-spray I tried hard very hard to look as super cool as I could, running around town with 'wanker' keyed into the side of my car – it really was impossible. I mean, what self-respecting person drives a Renault Twingo, anyway?

* * *

I was required to go to court for a second time. It came about after a few years of visiting a bizarre and manipulative family with two children. There were huge concerns from the off. The parents were essentially neglectful, which is why a judge, five years down the line, removed both children to the relief of all concerned. It sounds harsh to say that – and to read it, doesn't it?

I visited the parents, Michael and Denise, several times following reports of the eldest girl, Kelly, aged nine years, escaping from the home early morning, half-dressed in a nightie with school uniform on top. She would wait outside school. No one in her family had noticed her disappearance. However, after a series of such events, on arriving early, a teacher called her parents, again, to request that they come and collect their daughter to get her dressed, breakfasted and out again at the appropriate time for school. The teacher would call me on each occasion at the surgery to inform me as health visitor and, of course, the child's social worker.

Kelly's younger sister was Charlene, who failed to thrive at all points of her life. She was underweight and stunted in terms of height until she was removed, after which she blossomed. It is a truth that children, if emotionally deprived, fail to grow – they are not only skinny but physically shorter, too.

On various occasions, Charlene was seen repeatedly banging her head against the wall, shouting, 'I'm hungry!' The family support worker had witnessed this, as well as seeing Kelly go to a cupboard and fetch a bag of hundreds and thousands and voraciously devour them.

Michael, the dad, was a factory worker and mum Denise was a part-time secretary. Puzzlingly, neither had the capacity to parent effectively, despite appearing to be reasonably bright in other areas. There were all sorts of concerns and quizzical raising of eyebrows amongst us professionals who tried to work with them.

I was tasked with trying to understand what exactly was going on with meal times in the family, as neither child was growing. I lived in the same town – could I visit to witness, first-hand, the feeding of the children? We wanted to know, what was on offer? Did Kelly and Charlene just turn things down and muck about, or were they not being fed at all?

On this particular day, I knocked at the door but was pretty much told to go away. I persisted, and I got myself in by letting them know that social workers wanted me to be here. Both children had a quarter of a small fish paste sandwich each for lunch. Nothing else. I suggested that they might be offered something to supplement this, but that was it. We talked about how the children were failing to thrive – but it did not compute. We talked about money – was this an issue? They stated that their salaries were not quite enough to stretch things, and so financial help was offered under the terms of Section 17 of the Children Act 1989, which is where some assistance can be offered to a family when they're finding it difficult to make ends meet (budgets to cover this are very much depleted these days though, so it's not the resource it once was).

We then discovered that Kelly had started running away again and this was becoming a worrying habit. Who might she have gone to? Can you think of anyone to call? Nope. Sorry.

The girls fell further behind in terms of their development, with Charlene left in nappies for protracted periods, leaving her with severe and persistent nappy rash. Their speech failed to progress and their behaviour was odd. It was a huge worry. If I called at the house, Dad would shout to the children: 'Don't answer the door!' But they'd come to the letterbox, poking their fingers through the flap and peering at me despite the instruction. So the case eventually went to court, as the children continued to slide down the centile charts for weight – both were significantly delayed now.

There are huge inhibitors to removing a child from an abusive environment. Foster carers and placements are not exactly abundant, and are much sought after. Plus the thresholds are high and elastic, despite several million calls being made to social care UK-wide each year. There is always a concerted effort to keep a family together. Always. There are many ongoing conundrums and challenges to this noble aim, however. Not least that there are insufficient social workers, health visitors and related professionals on the ground to enact this vital work.

So the team involved professionally with this family were asked to attend the family court to give evidence. I have learnt now that court visits tend to involve much hanging around in a waiting area, then several trips to the cafeteria out of boredom and anxiety (which the caffeine exacerbates) followed by attendant excursions to the loo. It becomes a loop until, 'You're on! Judge is going to call you next.'

You're whisked into the stand, you do the swearing on the bible thing and then stare around you to clock the assembly of gowned barristers, as well as the parents. The Judge looms large and on high to the right with an array of flunkeys sitting in the rows below him.

On this occasion, the questions from the defence weren't as bad as predicted. I was asked to clarify my involvement; could I say what I was concerned about and why; did I trust the parents? If they were turning up late for school collection, what did I think they were doing? 'How would I know?' was my first thought. The judge pushed me a bit, as though he thought I could have some insight but was holding back.

Then the prosecution, who were meant to be on our side, proffered questions. Could I elaborate on the weight of the children and their development and demeanour? Fortunately, when in extremis, I have a scarily photographic memory which I don't seem to possess in everyday situations. It's almost like I'm wired for ridiculously atypical events.

I had memorised and could visualise their centile charts and developmental milestones and was able to explain those with ease. It wasn't particularly favourable for the parents, who by now were glaring and visibly wishing me away. I was able to give a detailed account of my input and I even later received a letter from the county solicitor thanking me for my 'valuable work and input'. Well chuffed.

I was dismissed, giving way to the family outreach worker who was grilled for hours. She worked much more closely and on a daily basis with the family, so it was necessary, unfortunately for her. She looked wrecked when she had finished.

The children were removed and it was sad – but it was right when all things were considered.

They were adopted together and have since done well.

Chapter Eight
The Recession

It was 2007 and, after being at the village surgery for almost a decade, I felt that I needed a new challenge, to be the 'new girl' again otherwise one can become a bit stale. I hadn't really used the master's in health policy, planning and financing that I had worked so hard to get at the LSE, either. Despite the noblest intentions, like so many, I quickly learnt that without extended family support, there is a choice that has to be made between career development and being a mum. My focus was always on the balance between my children and work as there was no back up team for us.

However, now the children were that bit older, I thought that maybe it was time to get to grips with this management thing. It felt like the next logical move. I thought I wanted, and needed, a new intellectual challenge. So I took a job in the seaside town of Weymouth, which was a totally different political landscape. I would be moving from a rural caseload to a densely populated, hugely deprived one.

As one of two team leads, I spent more time in an office providing support and leadership for a large team of health visitors. I was still dealing with mammoth and heart-rending child protection situations, domestic abuse, drug dealers, users, the grinding poverty that some of the families were subjected to, and the associated liaison and reports with social services, as I still had a caseload to run, but I was also trying to sort out management issues and attempting to cover the work of other health visitors who were absent due to sickness. The HR department was not terribly useful, directing us to 'page 56 of section 9' that we needed to adhere to.

My overwhelming thought was that I could do without this hassle. It was not a happy time and the constant pressure that resulted from trying to do the job with scant resources meant that six months later I gave up the role and returned to my first love as a front-line health visitor in this busy and challenging area. Full-time and max strength.

It was without doubt the right decision and I've never looked back. I had to have a talk with myself and ask, 'Are you prepared to defend the indefensible?' Sometimes, instructions come down from on high and managers have no choice but to 'suck it up'. I get that. But I figured that if I truly wanted to become part of a hierarchy, I had to take the 'joke' and sign up. I don't think I would have been very good at bollocking folk for having transgressed on something that I thought, considering what we had to deal with on a daily basis, was inconsequential. Like not having done some mandatory training update in a timely fashion, when there were multiple terrifying child protection situations going on at the same time.

The admin stuff, and of course, our visits, are captured online and are of paramount importance to managers. Child protection situations can be volatile, life-threatening and suddenly catastrophic. In which case, the question has to be asked, was anything not done that could have been? But when disaster is averted, or avoided, who actually knows or cares if something that might have gone horribly wrong actually didn't? How do you measure that?

Who can tell what could have happened if those exchanges between the health visitor and a client at the end of their tether had not taken place? Whether it's simply some kind words and reassurance, or organising some counselling and sleep support, or a well-timed food bank voucher when the cupboards are bare – these are the things that can bring people back from the edge.

So no, management was not for me. It lacked immediacy and impact, that spark of meaningful exchange. I was pretty rubbish at it, to be fair.

My six months working in management coincided with a very difficult time for us as a family. The plan had been for J. to take voluntary redundancy, have a two or three-month rest to reboot, then he would start looking again for a new position. The redundancy cash would enable the children to stay at their respective schools and we would carry on. God, no. He laughs at such plans, does he not?

In September 2008, Lehman Brothers went down the pan suddenly. Hmmm. What's this all about? There was something in the air and I was beginning to get jittery about J.'s search for work. It should have been a breeze, shouldn't it? He was a graduate, with huge and extensive experience in technology as a project manager in blue-chip companies. And yet his applications weren't getting any responses, let alone securing interviews. Various employment agencies would email with a vacancy, but it generally felt that it was either not a real job or that he was there to make up application numbers. Either way, there were remarkably few opportunities and things slowly dried up even further, until it dawned on us that he might never work again – he was 50.

Meanwhile, we were in pecuniary freefall. Oh my, and how we fell. The bank balance had gone from £3,000 to zero in an instant, when the monthly outgoings did what they did and went out. Mortgage, loan, credit cards, school bills, utilities, food, petrol, train travel. It vanishes with remarkable speed. This was surreal. The *Alice in Wonderland* rabbit hole came to mind. Often.

Only a matter of months before, we were both in full-time employment, earning well with our combined salaries, with two children in independent schools (which was where the money went). When the recession hit and J.'s job search proved fruitless, we realised that it would take only a few – surprisingly few – pay cycles to slide incredibly rapidly to oblivion. We tried to make sense of it.

A situation that at first had seemed so manageable and so temporary quickly started to seem desperate, like we had landed in another universe. There were hundreds of job applications made. Hundreds. Each made with care and hope that maybe this would be the one. J. would wave me off in the morning looking haunted – a shadow of himself. He was pretty much in denial and disbelief and not in the best frame of mind to apply, optimistically, for jobs.

Some family members said, 'There's work if you want it – plenty of jobs.' Those who had no experience of this and had never had to apply for work, of course. I accompanied J. to the nearest Tesco, where he asked the manager for an application form. The manager asked what his experience was. J. replied, 'IT project manager.' The manager looked embarrassed and asked him to complete the form and a psychometric test. J. ticked all the boxes for daytime work, night shifts – any shift at all, in fact. Never heard a thing. No acknowledgement or reply. Nada.

The same thing happened with Sainsbury's, the Post Office, several other retail outlets. Nothing. Someone in the village sidled up to me, slyly, in the dark one evening and said, 'Tell your old man I think he's lazy.' Christ alive. There are no words. I mean, what did we do to deserve this? (It was only later, after our recovery, that we learnt that in casual work, supermarket jobs, for instance, they wouldn't ever shortlist a previous manager or similar, as they knew that they wouldn't stay. So, no matter how much you wanted – no, needed that job, you were never going to be considered for it.)

The irony of spending my working day trying to help mothers to deal with crushing debt, and then returning to face our own money issues, was not lost on me.

You await the implosion, sick with anxiety and waiting for the Sword of Damocles to fall. Immediately before the descent, you look at the depleted bank account, and internally collapse. 'Money talks – it said goodbye,' as somebody once wisecracked. I tried to cut back on food, on cosmetics, anything I could, but the elephant in the room was the school fees. Now, please don't judge me for this. We really felt that we didn't have much option but to pay for the kids' education.

Some years back, while GG and BB were still at primary school, I had covered for another health visitor at a local school for an open health session – the pupils could come and talk to you about anything health-related in the youth club attached to the school, one lunch time.

I was visibly shocked when faced with a boy who, on discovering the new face at the nurse's desk, asked for directions to the toilet. Before I could reply, he informed me that he was going to piss in my office anyway. Charming. A gaggle of girls arrived to ask, earnestly, about quitting smoking. They were all of 13. We talked about giving up the cigs, but also their expectations and future educational aspirations. They genuinely looked baffled. There were none.

Another boy arrived, requesting condoms. I didn't have any because, even though I am a nurse, midwife and health visitor, I was deemed 'not qualified' to give them out. Don't ask. He said it would be my fault if he got his girlfriend pregnant tonight. I suggested that he kept it in his trousers until he had taken responsibility and purchased some himself.

Other girls came to peer through the office door window, which was adjacent to their youth club area where they played their music. My exchanges took place to the sound of some 'banging choons' – something to do with 'Muthafuckers'. It throbbed intrusively, with considerable volume and, thrillingly, on a loop. Departing the premises with a massive migraine, I muttered, 'Over my dead body will my children go there.'

It has to be said that the school had a 'good' Ofsted report at that time, and it might have been that my experience was not the typical display of behaviour which was described as 'satisfactory'. I have said that it might have been an 'off day' and had I visited on another day, my experience might have been entirely different. Who knows?

We just managed to fund places for the children to attend a local prep school and respective independent senior schools, largely from J's salary and some borrowing when the fees began to rocket. They had several happy years at their schools, until J. took voluntary redundancy.

But our present financial chaos meant we had to be grown up, take some very big decisions and talk to the schools involved. Suddenly we would no longer be considered stable or reliable, somehow. Possibly even to our own children. That we had been unable to secure their places for the rest of their education felt like a terrible failure. We were unable to protect them (which was patently untrue – but it really was how we felt).

Somehow, we managed to get BB through as he was about to complete A levels, but even with a decent scholarship, it was going to be impossible for GG, as she had some three years left. The headteacher of her school was decent but sombre, and said that she had to go. Brutal but honest. I cried and didn't stop for about a year. We had funded their education for 10 years: six years for BB and four for GG. It wasn't bad for my other half, who'd been given away by his birth parents in a girl's dress at six weeks old, and me, a girl who had to pee in a bucket as a child. But there we were: our luck had run out and we had to face it head on.

We applied to a grammar school in the next county, as GG had a good friend there, and what was really in short supply right now was a friend. She sat the exam and passed but it wasn't the usual time of year for admissions – so we still had to go for appeal. It was an unmitigated disaster.

J., prior to the appeal, indicated that he would 'lead' it. We sat together, nervous and dry of throat, several metres away from the panel of four in the usual, inhospitable, dusty hall, the teachers at one end, behind a long desk, and us at the other. Why did we want our daughter to attend this school?

J. started to speak, then faltered and unexpectedly started to cry. He turned to me and, through quiet, mangled vocal cords, said he couldn't do it. I stepped in. I was confused and unprepared for this emotional response from J. I knew he felt that he had let us all down but I hadn't seen him cry until now. At that point, I wanted it to stop but the panel didn't appear to be phased by his upset.

'We would like her to have a place at your school as she has a friend here,' I chirruped as confidently as I could. 'In view of having to leave her present school, she will be losing *all* of her friends and associates so it would be the most human thing to have at least one pal, wouldn't it?' No real response. Blank uncomfortable stares and legs shifting under their desk.

'How do you feel your daughter would benefit from being here? What would happen if she didn't secure a place here? We don't usually allow places to be allocated out of sequence and we don't usually take from the independent sector as a "priority".' The looks were knowing. Ah, yes, the private sector. The elephant in the room, again.

They considered us to be some kind of aristocracy... Perhaps, in their heads, we were Lord and Lady Featherstonehaugh and not considered human or worthy of any compassion, at all.

We had been pigeon-holed, incorrectly, but that's what happens. People love to put you in a box, don't they? Compassion and all the attendant feelings associated with humanity were reserved for others. We deserved our fall from grace – that was the clear impression. Perhaps we did, but did our daughter deserve to be treated as a pariah? I knew intuitively that they wanted me to grovel and say how much of a victim she was and how we were victims, too. I couldn't play the game though, and to GG's detriment.

The Recession

While checking J. for signs of complete breakdown or collapse, I proclaimed proudly that any school that our daughter attended should be glad to have her, and outlined all the things that she would bring to the school: she could play violin, piano, she could sing – grade 4 at the time. I knew I should play the victim card but, somehow, the opposite came out and I dug in.

The appeal had, of course, slipped away. In all likelihood, it had never been within our grasp. They started to smirk, just a little now, knowing I was rattled. 'Bollocks to you' was my considered demeanour from then on. Childish, I know, but it felt that everywhere we turned we were met with derision. They had no idea who we were and that our cottage was falling down in one section, that in order to send our children to their schools we drove a 'rip off' lease car via the NHS car scheme, and holidays were a long-distant memory. We were 'from the private sector' and, therefore, personas non grata.

I decided, way too late, that maybe I should allow for a little vulnerability, and informed them that J. had also passed his 11-plus, but that his adoptive parents had not taken his earned place, as the grammar school was five miles away. This meant buses, paying for the costly uniform and the whole thing was considered a bothersome inconvenience, so he was denied a place by his parents, who were surely there to make the best choices on his behalf – they had elected to adopt, after all. It was a decision that would impact his life forever, as he had had to undertake both his A levels and his degree as a mature student. Still, no response, no traction gained.

J. only discovered in his mid-forties about his denied grammar school place and was shocked, having had no clue beforehand. His adoptive father had said, casually, when we were talking about schooling for our two: 'Oh, you passed the 11-plus, you know.'

No, J. didn't know. 'What do you mean?' he asked.

'Well, you passed but only *just*, so we felt that it was best that you just stayed at the local school.' He laughed.

J. left the room and questioned everything. This cannot be right. What about the next people in the queue for adoption? Who were they? What were they like? Who were the couple who had taken the previous much-wanted and precious child from the unmarried mother's home? Perhaps he should or could have been placed with them? It all seemed like some monumental and unfathomable lottery, and here we were doing the same for our girl, for different reasons of course, but she would still be denied a place. Just like J. had been. We left crestfallen and defeated. We were exhausted and drained and just about had the money for the petrol to get home.

Someone from the panel phoned later that day and, as predicted, informed us that we had been unsuccessful in our appeal. We had been advised earlier, during the process, not to ask why. Of course I asked why. They didn't want to explain – it all felt a bit embarrassing for the member of the panel and we sank back into our despair. We had six weeks to secure her a school place somewhere.

A letter came from the other school we had applied to. The appeal date was set. We attended, got a grip and stated our case – less defensively, of course. It was my turn to cry this time. Just a bit of a chin wobble, and with a little choking on sentences I managed to hold it together. I said quietly that I just wanted her to be happy. The deputy head was sweet and understanding and I believe that he was genuinely touched by our situation. Our daughter was given a place. Thank you. So very much.

Meanwhile, the bank began to take the loan repayment out of my salary as soon as it hit our account, and claw back anything they could. We were left with even less money and couldn't plan for anything. Not even a weekly shop. I had to do everything possible to protect my salary – but how?

I quickly accessed the Citizens Advice Bureau in Weymouth, who advised that I set up a new and different bank account to receive my salary. Pronto. The new account would protect my salary and give us more power in terms of how it was spent. It was the beginning of our recovery, in that we had some stability – huge chunks of dosh could simply not disappear without any warning. Now we were in a position to plan and make decisions accordingly and negotiate the payback of debts incrementally and in manageable instalments.

I would scream and rant in the car when alone. Losing my shit. I would yell at God and politicians in particular. Scream therapy. Highly recommended. Do it in the car though – spare the neighbours.

What was strange was that to outsiders nothing much had really changed, but in reality, everything had. I could barely afford petrol now, even though my work depended upon it. In fact, my diesel lease car was particularly irritating: it was a whole 10p more expensive per gallon to fill up. And every single penny counted.

There were days when phone calls from creditors were never ending and relentless. The operators were sometimes kind and understanding, others were threatening and sinister. I have to say, most were kind. We negotiated a monthly repayment for each of our creditors and the haranguing phone calls stopped. The paper bills, which were now being paid by direct debit, would sometimes be piled on the kitchen table and then somehow migrate under the kitchen table but, essentially, we knew that all the debt was covered. Phew.

Some days, most days, I would purchase a 36p super-market family pack of own-brand scones before work and that would be my diet for the next few days. Half for breakfast, half for lunch, one pre-driving home (which was supper, because then I could feed the family and wouldn't be hungry), half for breakfast the following morning. Fuck it, I'll have a whole one. I got to hate that supermarket. And the scones. The phrase 'Let them eat cake' sprang to mind.

The financial crisis was in full swing by now, I was in the incongruous position of visiting families who were in exactly the same position. Dads, with little warning, were returning home, ashen-faced, with their redundancy letters. Or unemployed, despite endless applications. Out of work, out of hope and the cupboards bare. I would suggest that they might ask their mortgage provider for a mortgage holiday if that's what they were struggling with; I would advise writing to the CEO of the company as the responses we received always seemed to be more considered and sympathetic, rather than those of the lowly echelons who were often more brutal. I might also suggest an urgent appointment with Citizens Advice, and offer the tip on the changing of bank accounts, if they were struggling with their bank taking all available cash, as we had been.

I didn't let on to *any* of my clients that I was in the same position. I alluded to my insider knowledge having been gained through visiting 'others' who were going through the same thing. It is a well-known truth that some, but not all, clients believe that health visitors have not experienced real life at all. Again, we all make assumptions, don't we?

I worked with a GP at one point during this time who was married to another GP, and although delightful in very many ways, refused to give out food bank vouchers, proclaiming that people ought to budget according to their means. Ahem. This was coming from someone who didn't ever have to worry about being made redundant or paying their mortgage or anything pecuniary at all. Ever. Bless.

It was so reassuring to visit those who weren't struggling, sometimes. It felt that for those moments you were protected from having to confront this overwhelming and never-ending battle of awful deprivation. One family, most memorable as both parents worked at the bank that had been J.'s previous employer, appeared so safe and secure. They had their new lovely baby. Clearly there were no financial concerns. I would weigh their delightful, gurgling tot, plot weight on the centiles and enthusiastically reassure and congratulate mum on her parenting, discussing colic, safe sleep, emotional well-being and breastfeeding. They told me all was well for them. On leaving the warm, comforting blanket of their sanctuary, I wondered when, if ever, we would feel safe like that again.

'Sell your house,' one bank official barked when we were trying to extend an overdraft. When J. initially signed on for unemployment benefit, having never done it before, he was advised that, the following week, he wouldn't have to make the journey to sign on, having just completed the paperwork. It was our naïve belief that everyone said what they meant and meant what they said. Bearing in mind that with 38 years of paying tax and contributions, J. had roughly contributed half a million pounds to the Exchequer, possibly more, he was entitled to the princely sum of £64 per week for six months only – just over £4,000. That was it.

J. called the benefit office when his first payment had not been made. The advisor testily advised that he was meant to be there to sign in person so he would be sanctioned this week. No benefit for two weeks.

'What? There must be some mistake. I was definitely told I didn't have to come in,' he explained.

J. had to go in to the job centre to sort it out. We couldn't afford the train fare. He had to pay for his blood pressure medications this week – around £7 for each medication and he needed two types. In Scotland or Wales they would have been free. But we now were looking at going without food again – except for the children, clearly. Back to scones for breakfast, dinner and tea.

He made the £7.50 train journey to face the 'charms' of the advisor at the job centre, who was brutal and condescending. It's your own fault, basically.

'No one could have possibly advised you not to come in. What work are you looking for?'

'Well, I was an IT project manager,' he offered, cheerfully.

She sneered and made sure that he was not going to make the same mistake again. Phone calls were made. Go upstairs, they want to speak with you there. He waited for over an hour and then was sent back downstairs, where he waited for another hour, to be told he would not receive a payment this week in view of not coming in when he should have.

'Don't do this again,' he was told. 'Your wife is working, isn't she? Either she gives up work and you get the benefits available, or you sell your house or you find another job.'

I was having a coffee break at work one afternoon and realised that I was down to the last £5 in my purse – some insurance money that we were expecting to be credited didn't come in. That night after work, it was a toss-up between putting £5 of petrol in the car to ensure the 17-mile journey home – I was on the yellow light – or feed the children so they didn't go to bed hungry. I made a fraught and unsuccessful attempt at contacting a family member who might have been able to put some money into our account via the internet. She wasn't in.

Heart in mouth, I drove home on the 'bingo' light, expecting to run out of fuel at any point. I didn't have money for a mobile phone top-up or breakdown cover, so I'm not sure what I would have done if I had come a cropper. But my only option was to go for it.

The Gods were with me. I parked up at home in the hedge and jogged up to the local supermarket to purchase baked potatoes and beans all round. The eagerly anticipated cash was credited the following morning, so I could thankfully make the 17-mile journey back to work.

I was selling old LPs at the time to eke out our finances, to a shop near the surgery. There was also a cash-recycle shop where I could sell items such as PS2s, old mobiles, that sort of thing. I would scour the house for things to sell.

One week, we were particularly skint and I hesitantly took off my wedding ring and asked how much I would get for it. I placed it on the weighing scales. £12. I grimaced and flinched, simultaneously. It's 18 carats, I protested. No it's not, it's nine. It's 18, I snapped, glaring at him, snatching it back, annoyed and ashamed in equal measure that I had contemplated selling it. I replaced it on the third finger of my left hand. For better or worse. This was worse than anything I had anticipated, for sure.

J. had applied to a nearby tourist attraction, a castle, where he got a job selling tickets and parking cars at weekends. That was all he could secure. From managing multi-million pound budgets to this. Christ. Some friends who had known us through the lucrative years said on his first morning, when I really could have done with a friendly, 'It'll be OK – it's just a blip,' joked: 'Let's go over to the castle and laugh at J.'

We really learnt who our friends were. In truth, we were shocked at how thoughtless, and worse, some people could be. What was most surprising, though, was the kindness of people who we didn't know very well, but who helped us tangibly to get through. Thank you so much. You know who you are.

We got into some ridiculously weird and niche situations. My lease car, for example. The lease was about to expire and we definitely needed a car; it was impossible to do without when GG's school was 11 miles away and work was 17 miles each way.

But I had not claimed the mileage – yes, stupidly, I know, but it was a few pence per mile –and now it was impossible to prove how much mileage I had done with any accuracy. I provided a guesstimate and the lease manager unhelpfully decided that I didn't do enough mileage to warrant a new lease car. Okaaaay. So now I won't be able to afford any car to get me to work to pay the bills or take GG to school. Now we were well and truly stuffed. It looked as though I might have to give up work, even though I was really the only one earning, because we were trapped in this bizarre scenario of my not being able to actually get there.

The Recession

I think it's worth pointing out here how time-consuming being poor is. You have to think about every single detail of your entire life at every single decision point and at multiple points during each and every day. Can I afford to pay for GG's school trip? No, because she needs new school shoes. (I even, embarrassingly, haggled in a well-known chain store for a pair of shoes for her. GG was mortified as I came off second best. 'We don't do market stall trading here,' came the snooty reply.) What about the milk bill? Can I afford some fresh meat and veg this week? Or is it store cupboard items only? When does the next tranche of money come in? Friday? Ah, so I will fill up with petrol, then, and not go into town on the Saturday to preserve fuel for work on Monday, leaving enough in the account for the train fare J. needs to go and sign on. Then it's only two weeks until payday, so we can eke out the remaining dosh on beans, bread, take sandwiches or scones for lunch; the dog needs vaccines but we'll delay those until next month. Oh, and GG needs a top-up on her phone, so if I go without food again, I can organise that… and BB needs a haircut, but does that leave us with enough cash for J.'s blood pressure meds?

It's a constant and relentless cycle of thinking ahead, adding up small sums in your head, and just trying to survive, the likes of which, when there's always sufficient resources in one's account, are unknowable and beyond comprehension.

It's like the puzzle of a Rubik's cube, where the colours never line up, no matter how hard you try. The kids got used to the reality of our new existence and were incredibly brave and resilient. They remain so. I am so bloody proud of them.

I had a meeting with a manager to discuss the car situation. She was originally scratchy with me. I plonked my scales, my hearing testing equipment and my own rucksack on the floor and asked about the policy re lease cars – how could I continue to work when my husband was now unemployed and we couldn't afford to purchase any car of any persuasion? Why does the lease car policy apply in this way? The job requires a car.

'I can't do it without one,' I said, pointing at the baggage on the floor.

'Why *have* you brought all your stuff along?' she asked, staring at my bags.

'Because another manager said that I could walk my patch, which extends over a 10-mile area in each direction, so if I have a visit down in the town centre and then my next one is back up on the edge of Bournemouth, what do I do then? And how do I get to work anyway, which is 17 miles from home?'

After her initial briskness with me, she suddenly halted – asking where the conversation was going. 'Is this a grievance?'

We stared at each other. I thought she was about to dismiss me or similar and replied, 'No, it's not a grievance. I'm asking for your help.'

With that, she visibly mellowed, sinking back in her chair. She actually bloody softened! This hard-nosed manager, who probably didn't come across the likes of me every day, thawed immediately. She offered to ask the leasing manager to extend the lease. I said that I had tried, but that the price had rocketed from £300 per month to a ridiculous £500 and we couldn't stretch to that. She asked me about the situation in more detail. She said she would really try to help and would get back to me personally. It was strange to see, and heart-warming somehow that I had really got through to her. Sadly it didn't help, but at least she tried.

Some acquaintances who were parents to a friend of my daughter got to hear of our situation and stepped in with a small loan, which we paid back in instalments every month. We purchased a really old Mercedes, as I was advised that they ran and ran and so wouldn't need much in way of maintenance. We were so beyond grateful. Somehow, by the skin of our teeth, and with very little sanity left, especially for J., we got through.

He was still at the castle but was considering teaching maths. He had always liked the subject, had maths A level and, being a graduate, he successfully applied for a trainee maths teacher position at a local comprehensive on the graduate training programme – the one where you learn in the school environment. He did a week to see if he liked it. He did, though in truth he didn't have much choice.

I would give him a lift to work so we wouldn't need a second car, nor would it involve a train fare. It was brilliant to have a regular income again. It wasn't what he had earned before, but the predictability was a huge relief and we could plan our finances accordingly. It also meant growing confidence again for J. There was a marked sense of pride returning and he didn't look so defeated and hunted.

I would collect him from his school at the end of the day. He would stay on until I could get there at around 5.30 each day, then have tea and toast on returning home and start planning lessons and marking homework. He'd continue until 10 or 11 o'clock on most days. Every day, in reality. It was almost five years since we had had a holiday, and years since we'd eaten out or bought new clothing.

Our first Christmas in this situation was abysmal. The turkey was abandoned for a cheap Bulgarian goose from a dodgy outlet which, when cooked, smelt weirdly of chemicals. I checked to ensure that I had removed the bag of giblets. Yep, I really had. It tasted of burnt creosote. Christ, was it really a goose? What kind of unidentified beast was this? I don't think we'll ever know. We laughed. The presents were sparse and one of them to my daughter was unwrapped, which she still teases me about now.

The worst part was that, almost six months later, in the pile of undisturbed letters under the table, we found an envelope that would have transformed that Christmas and beyond. The dog had been sleeping on it for months under the kitchen table. In our sad and hopeless demeanour – I believe that we had been depressed – we had ignored things.

I opened it – it was from the Inland Revenue. Oh, God, what do they want? Out came the letter with a perforated edge three quarters of the way down with the sum of £3,000 written on it. Another bill, I thought. Can't we catch a break? How are we going to pay that?!

I called J. and began to wail, when suddenly it dawned on me that it wasn't a bill at all, but a cheque, and made payable to him. It was always people demanding money, so this was a miracle. Christ, I had to pay it in pretty damn quick – it had been sat there for five months, three weeks and four days, and would expire in three days! I cut off the call to him saying I would explain later and sped off to Dorchester to pay it in, stat. It was a sad state of affairs that I didn't even recognise a cheque when I saw one.

We were glad to be surviving. J. was beginning to look tired again but he was grateful for the job. The pupils were sometimes challenging and he wasn't the best in terms of instilling fear into them. Others had the knack and could walk into a room to instant silence. With J. they were on their phones chatting, texting, creating all sorts of havoc. Then, the month of his qualification, he applied for a position back at his original place of work, where he had been before the recession.

He was shortlisted. Could it be true? Dare we dream that he might return? It was tense: there was the initial interview, a telephone interview with a senior executive and an HR interview. With each step, there was more and more riding on it. He looked haunted again, knowing and feeling the magnitude and gravity of the situation. After the interview he said he had done his best. He couldn't have done any better. Without meeting my eyes, he said, 'I don't know what to do if I don't get it.'

Amazingly, he secured the position. He was earning more than he had earned beforehand, which was surreal, and much more than he was earning as a trainee teacher. Phew. It was a hell of a ride but we got there.

I used to purchase a coffee from Caffè Nero most mornings pre-recession, but this was a habit that had to be broken, and fast. I'd swiftly halted every kind of frivolous purchase. When

I next ventured in, many months later, to purchase a cappuccino as a proper treat, I was greeted by the young barista who I had got to know a little prior to the tightening of belts. He was cross with me.

'Oh, I see,' he said, 'the queue at Costa was too long this morning, was it?'

I turned around, thinking he was speaking to someone else. No, he definitely meant me. 'Oh, no, not at all.' I didn't really know what to say, so I just said the truth of the matter: 'I haven't been able to do my usual things for ages, like getting a coffee, for instance. My husband was made redundant, you see. Things changed a lot for us.'

He looked shocked, he visibly reddened and said, 'I didn't realise. I thought you'd gone elsewhere – I feel guilty now.'

'It's OK, you weren't to know.'

I have never taken anything for granted again since then. Ever. The fact that I can put petrol in the car. The shopping. The trips paid for the children. Putting them through university. Paying for all sorts of things. Bills. Meals out. Holidays occasionally. It all makes me smile and feel immense gratitude to those who helped us. To others who found themselves in this situation and survived: I salute you. For those who didn't, I salute you too. It could have been absolutely any of us. Be kind... You know the rest.

A month later, J. noticed the unkind woman from the benefits office at one of the stations en route to work one morning. She was running along the platform, out of puff, trying to access a push-button entrance to his carriage. The train was stationary, but the doors had just closed. He swiftly pushed the button from inside, preventing her from boarding. She gave up, clearly furious, turning her back on the train. Yes! Imaginary fist bump. Payback time. Permit us just a little gloat. Memo – don't try to diminish someone when you are in a position of power; you never know how temporary your authority might be.

*   *   *

Meanwhile, back at my place of work, I was visiting a single mum who was teetering on the verge of losing her children. On one particular morning I attended the conference detailing the bewildering circumstances of Gina and her two children, and her attempts to hang on to them despite neglecting them in order to go out drinking. She would leave them with a variety of acquaintances, one of whom was an elderly female who'd had her own children removed historically, yet was willing to babysit for a few quid.

The youngest child, Laura, aged 20 months, was mostly still fed on formula milk and put to bed at 4pm every day.

Unsurprisingly, as she was neglected and unstimulated, she couldn't stand, cried relentlessly, was underweight and her development was delayed across the board.

The older one, Bobby, aged three, was damaged too. When I last saw him, at the most recent core group meeting, with the other professionals involved and Gina with her children, he had hit me when I attempted to thwart his exit from the meeting room. Gina scooped him up and calmly removed him from the proximity of the door, but Bobby came back for more. I held the door shut but got a good kicking to the shins for good measure. Often, when the social worker and I visited Gina's home, Bobby would be naked, even in the depths of winter. There were soiled nappies on the floor and the last vestiges of long abandoned takeaways with the attendant empty cans of special brew.

I had submitted my report two days before the conference. Each report outlines not just the basic information, such as names, dates of birth, NHS number, address, but also has to detail the reason for the initial conference − the ongoing concerns that outline why we had to step in. In Gina's case, the worry was that she was living a chaotic life of drink and drugs with an abusive male − not the father of the children − and the house was pretty squalid, which was affecting the children, who were often ill with diarrhoea and vomiting.

My report outlined a chronology of our input and visits, the health status of each child, each parent (if known – in this instance the father had disappeared and was unknown), the parenting capacity of each parent and any risks therein.

We also have to detail what is positive about the situation, analyse the overall picture and make recommendations for a sustainable and workable plan going forward – something that will ensure the safety of the children and address the behavioural changes that the parent(s) will have to make to protect and prioritise their children – although this of course has to be realistic. We might get the mother and/or father to attend a parenting course, or maybe they need some mental health support, particularly if they themselves have been victims of historical abuse. Or a family support worker could be involved – someone who visits the family at home intensively, to work with them on budgeting skills, managing bedtimes, improving on cooking skills and similar. It really depends on the specific concerns with each situation.

Today was going to be tough, as Gina was quite pissed off and vocal about her children being subject to a Child Protection Plan. She was a good parent, it was all our fault, she had been depressed, she couldn't remember all the appointments she had to take the children to... But she also argued noisily with other parents in the street and at school, and we had recently been informed that she had been thrown out of a fish and chip restaurant in the town precinct late at night for having casual sex on one of the pleather banquettes, whilst everyone else at the front of the shop tried to enjoy their catch of the day.

I got to the conference room at the local office and, after much hanging around in reception, was buzzed up and allowed entry by one of the admin girls. We are always imbued with a sense of jangly nerves and anticipation on arrival. Often, parents and other family members are aggressive, because they are frightened to be faced with what feels like 'authority'. It becomes a stark reality that the state with all its monolithic powers is kicking in and they could, at some point, be involved with a legal battle if they don't change. And repeated patterns of behaviour are often hard-wired and manifestly difficult to change.

Faced with a selection of professionals with whom we share the protagonist, we puzzle over why we have never met or communicated with any of them before: police, team managers, teachers, deputy heads, outreach workers and today... ta-da! There was a GP. Blimey! Although they have to supply a detailed report, they rarely attend. Only the most committed do that.

I asked breezily if the admin team had received my emailed report, which was usually printed off times 10 and in a neat pile, ready for each professional to read and digest prior to beginning the conference, so that we all understood the bigger picture and were aware of the most recent events before the meeting got underway.

However, today the piles of reading material were absent.

'Computers are down so we haven't received any reports. You're going to have to either rely on memory, or if you have your own copy then you will have to read it out.'

Brilliant.

I selected my seat, put my work bag on the appropriate section of the communal desks/tables arranged in a square, poured myself a tumbler of water, offering to do the same for others.

It was likely to be feisty. Gina was at the end of a long, drawn-out legal battle. The judge at the last court hearing had got her measure, asked her to take note of the social worker's recommendations and adjourned for the next sitting, which would be next week. She was likely to lose her children.

'Is Gina here?' someone chirruped.

'Not yet,' the team manager retorted. 'No idea if she's coming, to be fair; she was in a strop yesterday and she wouldn't say.'

'What about her mother?'

'Oh Christ, the last time Granny came, she hollered and accused and kicked the chairs over; she was clearly on something. The chairperson, Nick, had to warn her that he wouldn't put up with it.'

Granny was jittery and agitated, and had eventually quietened only after the threat to halt proceedings. Her drug of choice was amphetamines, so that was the most likely culprit.

At that point, a clerk popped in, buzzing open the door to say that both Gina and her mother were downstairs. Fingers crossed for a speed-free granny.

At these conferences, the independent chair – the person who conducts and leads the conference – starts the introductions, where we all state our names and roles, going around the table. The chair does most of the questioning and asks each professional in turn to outline their thoughts and interventions and analysis. We can all ask questions as we go along including, obviously, the family. The conference is an open and fairly free-flowing exchange, but if professionals go off at a tangent or if family members get abusive it is the duty of the chair to rein them in. Sometimes, things get so heated that proceedings have to be halted, but this only happens rarely.

Lots of issues are discussed – is the family feeding the children? Are they attending school? Being taken and collected on time? Are the parents still engaged in drug-taking activities? What is the evidence surrounding this? Are they engaging in any of the therapeutic courses that have been arranged? Are they engaging with professionals? Have they been threatening to professionals? How are the parents coping? Mental health? Are there any other inhibitors to behavioural change and how might the family address these? Can we help financially? There are many, many factors to consider and address.

There are often advocates made available if a family member has any learning difficulties to help them navigate the meeting. Someone who can halt the proceedings and ask, 'Do you understand that question?' Someone who can reframe a situation on behalf of the family concerned. Interpreters are made available if English is not the first language, and signers if a client is deaf.

Towards the end of the conference, when everything has been addressed and all the facts laid before us, the question is asked: should these children be subject to a Child Protection Plan? If so, under what category? Physical, emotional, sexual abuse? Neglect?

Today's chair, Vicky, murmured to the long-suffering social worker, Tanya, to acknowledge that they would both greet Gina and her mother to outline the proceedings and the content of the reports. There should be no surprises. If they were unhappy about the content of any professional's report or, indeed, anyone's input, this was the time and arena to address it. Historically, we attending professionals took our seats in the conference room and the family would enter afterwards – now we are instructed to wait in another room whilst the family enter the conference room first and we arrive after them, so that they, the family, don't feel that they are entering to a sea of often unfamiliar faces, making it an even more stressful occasion than it already is.

Gina and her mother had arrived. They both wore freshly laundered jeans and whilst Granny wore her usual hoody, Gina wore a baby pink rib-knit jumper. She looked smart and I felt that she had tried to make an effort. Her hair was scraped back into a low bun. The aroma of tobacco wafted in with Gina – maybe it was a ciggie to steady her nerves, maybe – but she was, sadly, angling for an argument.

She talked over everyone and accused us all of letting *her* down, despite the fact that she had roundly ignored all of the advice she had been given. In her defence, it must be scary being faced with all manner of folk all at once. I realised that the situation was overwhelming for her. The social worker with the patience of a saint was exasperated, and had been giving heavy hints that she would, in all likelihood, lose her children if she did not take responsibility for changing her 'hectic' lifestyle.

There had been much partying, with crates of lager seen being brought into her barely furnished flat on a Friday afternoon. Yet there was no bedding on the children's beds, and bluebottle flies lazily hung around the floor knowing that there were rich pickings for them in the barely hoovered, food-stained, shag-pile rug.

Gina obfuscated, blamed and cursed.

It was everyone else's fault that she had no food in the fridge for the children and no electricity to power the fridge anyway. Money would be found for weekend drinking and entertaining a string of casual boyfriends; Bobby would shyly tell his pre-school teacher, 'I've got a new daddy' only for the love interest to leg it after a weekend, never to be seen again.

Gina was actually bright and likeable, and had lots of potential, but had clearly experienced some kind of abuse or neglect herself, which very often, though not always, permeates and ripples through subsequent parenting. It was so sad that it had come to this.

We needed to impart some new information to Gina: the social worker had received several anonymous telephone calls from people concerned about her parenting, and these had to be followed up. The callers stated that they were worried about the youngest child's health as she always seemed to be hungry and crying and was delayed in terms of development.

Gina did not have the time to stay, however. The conference wasn't going her way. She had an appointment with the benefits office (we later found out that she didn't) and had to take one of her children to the GP surgery (that one was true). The children remained subject to a protection plan.

A court appearance was scheduled for the following week. Gina failed to turn up and so another date was set for the week after. Both children were removed and were placed with an aunt, who agreed to accommodate them and parent them going forward for as long as was required.

Gina flipped and freaked at their removal. She went full-on crazy and understandably so. There was talk of her hitting the drink and drugs hard. She was actively encouraged to have supervised access to her children, but she stopped turning up. And then nothing. A roaring silence. Had she moved? What had happened? We didn't hear from her for an eternity.

But then, having not done so for weeks, she started turning up to see her kids at the contact meetings. Gina began to take more of an interest in 'being there', as in not just going through the motions, but actually engaging in their wellbeing, their care, enjoying them. There were steps made to learn how to cook, actively supported by a family outreach worker, and she cleaned up her house. Bins were emptied and surfaces cleaned. Even the grass at the front, perennially unkempt and neglected, began to neaten. The family outreach worker had imbued Gina with a sense of what was necessary to run a home that was befitting of two children and, more importantly, a safe and contented family and a less chaotic life.

Gina began to have her children unsupervised – small steps at first, not always going well. But she took control and, with the help of a counselling service, and commitment to some cognitive behaviour therapy (CBT), she began to feel less vulnerable if the kids were out of control. It made her anxious when she thought that others were judging her – historically, she had lashed out, but now she felt more reassured that it was OK to ignore the opinions of others whose opinions had not been sought.

We applied for some new beds from a charity, which were granted. Gina began to be more assertive and less aggressive. She undertook the Incredible Years Parenting course – 12 weeks of diligent study, learning how to be more child-centred and engaged. It was hard and she often felt like giving up, but one day I saw her in the post office nearby and she had been purchasing some bedding for the children, which hitherto had never been a priority. She said, 'What choice do I have? I have to do this. I lost them once – I can't lose them again.'

She was right. This was her opportunity to get it right. It was about committing to the children and living life believing that she could change. Drink and drugs were replaced with routine and reading and playing. She was alone, but she was doing it. Auntie Susie was on hand in a practical way – she had always offered before, but Gina had refused help for fear of being seen as not coping. Granny was still not always a helpful influence, but Gina learnt to keep her at bay.

Parties were of the jelly and ice cream variety, rather than the vodka and White Lightning type. Budgeting and managing money were a breeze by now. Gina actually began to save. She had sorted out an arrangement to repay debt. And then she announced that she wanted to return to college and study childcare, which she did. God, there was no stopping her. There were incredulous faces and cynical shakings of the head, but off she went. The college organised some childcare for her. Her auntie helped financially in a small way – and very occasionally. Gina had taken the stabilisers off and was pedalling toward self-reliance and providing a stable environment for her children.

There were now no 'new daddies' around. Instead she described them as 'shit bags'. 'Who needs 'em? I'd like someone to share the kids with, sometimes, who wouldn't? But I'm not letting just anyone in – there's too much at stake. I'd rather be on my own,' was her considered judgement.

Wow. She had come such a long way.

I think, in truth, Gina was brighter than she thought, and it took a while for her to believe in herself and the prospect of change. She felt that she hadn't possibly lived up to her true potential and that if she lost the children for good, then all would be lost – it would be a totally damning indictment, one that would be too much to bear. So she eventually engaged with all the therapeutic interventions that were offered, made herself vulnerable and open to change. Sometimes, just sometimes, it all works, and the parent understands the magnitude of what's required and, rather than running in the opposite direction, is not scared by the process, but embraces it.

* * *

It is widely known that experience of traumatic events in childhood can have a profound adverse impact on brain development, leading to both physical and behavioural changes as the child tries to adapt to a stressful situation. These 'adverse childhood experiences' (ACEs), as they are known, that impact a child's emotional landscape include verbal, physical, emotional and sexual abuse, neglect, parental separation, household mental illness, domestic abuse, alcohol/drug abuse and imprisonment of a family member.

If trauma occurs over a prolonged period, it can harm the child's internal stress system, which then contributes to physical and mental health problems over a lifetime, making children more prone to problems with regulating their emotions. It is often linked to difficulties with behaviour such as attention deficit hyperactivity disorder (ADHD). The current thinking is that if you can get language development and self-regulation correctly sorted by the time a child attends school, almost everything else flows from that.

There is increasingly strong evidence about the 'first 1,001 days of life' – so from conception to when a child is two – and the impact this period has on future health and wellbeing. Babies and very young children who don't receive the care they need, for whatever reason, are much more likely to suffer problems as they grow up. So interventions from health professionals at an early stage can help improve children's current and future health. Research has shown that, along with longer-term benefits to wellbeing, visits from health visitors within those crucial first 1,001 days can save the NHS money, as problems can be solved before they escalate and become more complex.

But despite this evidence, we have to undertake just five visits in the course of a child's first two years. (Though in Northern Ireland, health visitors do seven visits, in Wales nine visits and in Scotland they do eleven.)

Whether the mother gets any further support beyond these five visits is very much down to our initial assessment. If we don't pick up any concerns from the off, new mums can go without the help they need, unless they present themselves to us at a later date, by which time they may well be in a crisis. And, of course, things change.

The first time we meet a new mum is when we arrange an antenatal visit at around 34 weeks of the pregnancy to discuss preparations for your new baby and your new life. Health visitors see you at this time to assess how your life is going before the baby arrives, so that we can establish a baseline of mood and a history. Have there been any mental health problems, physical health issues, how do you feel about being pregnant? How was childhood for you? Was there any abuse of any kind? Is there a history of self-harm? What are your housing conditions? Is your housing stable? Social networks? History of domestic abuse (we only ask if the mother-to-be is alone), learning difficulties? Do you work? Are there any complicated immigration issues? Any other responsibilities?

We have to be mindful that some might be reluctant to disclose any of the above if we have only just met, so often, as our relationship evolves, we get to know a little more of your hinterland.

Attachment is also discussed. Sue Gerhardt writes beautifully about this in her book *Why Love Matters*. She outlines why love shapes a baby's brain – particularly the social and emotional development. Our earliest relationships shape the baby's nervous system. So health visitors discuss with our clients the importance of holding their babies, gazing at them, interacting and cooing and chattering to them – holding them and loving them just because you can. Loving relationships are pivotal to the development of baby's brain and early interactions can have lasting consequences.

All being well, the next time we see you is for the new birth visit – between day 10 and day 14 after baby is born. This is where we assess baby's development and your mental health, undertaking baby's hearing test. We go over safe sleep and what it entails, discuss relationships, money, claiming benefits, remind you about registering the birth, identify extended family support. Do you know where your nearest child health clinic is? Do you know who to call at night if you're worried?

Sometimes, we ask the 'magic question'. If we could wave a magic wand, what would you want right now? Most replies revolve around 'more money', 'a new house', 'a new partner'. A few reply with a jaunty, 'David Beckham would sort out all three.' But just sometimes this unlocks a 'magic answer' that reveals something the family is struggling with but might not know how to tell us.

If you have a regular income and/or family support, plus an absence of drink/drugs/violence/mental health issues, you probably won't see us again (unless you want to come into the clinic) until the baby is around six weeks old.

The six-week contact is where we weigh and measure baby again to ensure appropriate growth and development, talk about safe sleep again and ask about support in an ongoing sense. Are there any issues worrying you? Lack of sleep? It will get better, I promise – just lend yourself to the chaos for a while; a kind of routine does emerge, honest. Are you remembering to eat? Drink? Is anyone hurting you? This has to be asked sensitively and usually when alone, for obvious reasons. Do you have an appointment with your GP for a check for you and baby?

If a mum appears to be confident and competent – as most are – then that family is categorised as 'universal'. They will still receive the 10-month and two-year developmental assessments – this latter check is often undertaken by the lovely community nursery nurse (CNN) in our area. If they decide they want any more input from a health visitor – for example, advice on feeding – they will need to seek this at the optional weekly baby clinic which runs rain or shine, with the exception of Christmas and New Year's Day. In truth, it's often busy and noisy, which can be a real barrier to an open and in-depth conversation. You can always call us, though, and we can organise a home visit if something is not going well for you.

Families might require more visits because of a suspected low mood or a feeding issue – cow's milk protein allergy, for instance – and this means that they would be in receipt of the Universal Plus service. This is where we provide some ongoing input by bringing other relevant services together to meet a family's more complex needs.

The issue with basing the system around just five 'contacts' is that many families could easily need further input at any time, but if everything is OK at the new birth visit, they are just assigned the universal package. In reality, however, they may be sitting quietly at home going round the bend. In other words, unless we get to follow our own professional instinct or to think autonomously – which the 'targeting' of our clients deliberately inhibits – we could be missing someone who needs more support.

Unless of course we just go guerrilla and visit anyway. Yep, done that.

Chapter Nine
Please Don't Feed the Trolls

As I enter Alice's house, the stench overwhelms me. I am dry heaving behind my hair and trying to hide my retching as I extend the usual salutations. She has two children: one aged 14 years, Lucy, and an 18-month old child, Charlotte. The place is filthy; I don't say that lightly. Unemptied cat litter trays, bins overflowing, food trodden into the carpets and furniture ingrained with the last vestiges of food. Everywhere there are piles of discarded takeaway cartons and teetering mountains of body-odoured, unwashed clothes.

The most potent aroma emanates from Alice herself. She was in care for most of her life, almost certainly abused, and we have been told that this was her only defence – a form of armour. This single-parent family's case has been closed by social care and they have been deemed to be coping.

In addition to the smell and the dirt, no one has any bedding. There are several kittens skittering hither and thither, a mad Jack Russell and a depressed chinchilla. After being invited to take a seat on one of the sofas, one of the kittens climbs onto my lap, making its way onto my shoulder and finally into my freshly highlighted locks. I hear myself say aloud, 'I wonder if someone could be so kind as to remove this kitten from my hair?'

I visited Alice because another professional had called the office to say they were concerned that the home conditions were bad. They could have and should have called social care themselves but often they don't want the responsibility of being identified as the person who referred them, so they pass it to us. On stepping into Alice's house, I knew that I had to get her back under the social care umbrella.

The previous health visitor had been visiting for a while, but had got stuck, in the sense that she was not effecting any change. In these instances, we ask if we can swap such clients, in order to bring a fresh energy and perspective to the situation.

Today's level of neglect was unacceptable. Neglect is defined as the ongoing failure to meet a child's needs. There is a tool called the Graded Care Profile which we use to make our assessments. The profile looks at the impact the level of neglect has. Does the child regularly get ill with diarrhoea and vomiting, adversely impacting their health? Is there any negativity or criticism meted out by the parent that is impacting the child's self-esteem? Is there decent food, regularly provided? Is good behaviour rewarded?

The tool highlights the strengths, the weaknesses and, ergo, what is good and what needs to be changed. It also helps to evidence the degree of neglect and therefore makes it harder for social care to pronounce that a family is functioning when it's clear that they are not.

Health visitors have to look at the family's living situation and make a judgement. A mild level of grubbiness might constitute a concern if it remained unaddressed or worsened, but it's not the same as a home that, say, has dog shit all over the floor with no attempts to clean up. By working out what the issues are, we can identify what support to put in place to remedy the situation. Hopefully.

The first arena we assess is the physical – the quality of food, clothes and health. Well, in this instance, the clothes for Lucy, Alice's 14-year-old, were always stained, grubby and ill-fitting. Summer clothes were in use during winter months. The toddler, Charlotte, was often grubby too, but so are most 18-month-olds. The food was cheap, of low quality and low nutrition which, to be fair, is often the way when we are short of money. The children's health was often compromised due to the regular bouts of diarrhoea and vomiting and there were a lot of cat and dog faeces around. So we're scoring pretty high here.

Charlotte had a bare cot/bed and there was an absence of sheets and bedding on Lucy's bed. Just a collection of clothes on a bare mattress and the usual variety of graffiti on the walls. 'Fuck off' is quite often written on walls or doors inside a home – more than you would think.

Safety is the next arena we look at, checking out how safe the home is and how able the older children are to keep themselves safe. Lucy had, allegedly, had sex with a man with learning difficulties she had met at the nearby hostelry, persuading him that she had gotten pregnant nine months after the event by borrowing a friend's child, parading it to him and extorting £100 out of him to stop her from reporting it to the Child Support Agency (CSA).

The next area is emotional health – how is the relationship between the child and their carer or parents? This wasn't *so* bad. Mum did demonstrate warmth and affection toward Charlotte, though she was quite cold and distant toward Lucy. Alice had maternally checked out, due to the long-held fallacy that they don't need you as much as the 'young' child. This is patently incorrect. They often need you more. Issues such as emotions, school, homework, relationships, friends, worries, careers advice, the future – just knowing that you are emotionally available is important.

The final area is developmental: are the children encouraged to learn and praised when they demonstrate doing something well? Or, as with some parents, do they dismiss, scorn or berate even when something noteworthy has occurred?

The bottom line was that, after going through the assessment, there was hardly overwhelming evidence that mum was coping in terms of caring and it gave me the evidence I needed to go back to social care to say, 'You've got this wrong. There is still ongoing neglect and I have evidence that it's not gone away.'

Meanwhile, I had become puzzled about another woman who had, hitherto, readily allowed me to visit her and her baby but was avoiding me now, despite knocking at her door and leaving her lots of written messages.

I called round one morning and she poked her head out of the top-floor flat living room window. She told me she couldn't see me today: 'I'm fine, just a bit under the weather.' She started to close the window but I felt there was something more. I shouted up that I wasn't going anywhere so she had better let me in. I was bluffing of course, but I wondered if she really wanted me to be firmer. She did.

She crept down the stairs and opened the front door about five inches. It appeared that it couldn't be opened any further. I asked her what was troubling her and suggested that perhaps in sharing it, it might not be so overwhelming. She was stalling still. I persisted and she tentatively let me in.

I had to fight my way in. There was a fortress of rubbish behind the door which prevented it from opening fully. I pushed my way through and found the stairway and entire flat littered with black bags, clothes, vodka bottles, food remains, takeaways, beer cans, baby clothes; it looked like a shocking Channel Four programme about hoarders. I couldn't leave her like this, so I asked if she wanted help to clean up. It wasn't possible to live and parent and cook and do all the usual things in this condition.

I went to the corner shop for cleaning products (purchased with my own money) and black bags and together, after several hours, we had licked it into shape. There was a lot of chucking out and, eventually, surfaces began to reappear and crockery and cutlery were replaced back in drawers and cups and glasses on shelves. Her daughter was at her mother's house, so this enabled us to crack on.

No amount of professional training for the post of health visitor can prepare you for moments such as this – it's not in the job description either. But countless health visitors up and down the country might be helping young mums like this from losing everything – all for want of some cleaning supplies and a helping hand.

Health visitors tend to need to be in possession of good humour, and often at our own expense. While on a visit to attempt to understand why a young woman had left her five-day old baby with an elderly grandfather to jet off to Majorca for an indeterminate number of days, I lowered myself onto the arm of the adjacent sofa to appear more accessible and less threatening. It tipped up. A combination of hefty arse and shabbily constructed sofa, methinks. Less DFS and more FFS, under the circumstances. I hadn't been invited to sit down, so it serves me right.

I visited daily to ensure that baby was being adequately fed and cared for until Majorca Girl returned after a week in the sun. She carried on with the care of her new baby as though nothing had happened. 'What's all the fuss about?' was the prevailing family opinion – 'I had a great time, it was booked long ago when I wasn't pregnant, so stop coming here upsetting the apple cart.' And the bloody sofa. She had a point.

All I could do going forward was make some visits to ensure that there were no more incidents of a neglectful manner, and that baby was being fed and was growing and cared for in an appropriate and loving way. Sometimes, it's about monitoring a situation. Even if, often, families don't want you to 'monitor', so you have to use all your skills to get in and make the necessary assessments.

A sense of humour is useful for all sorts of mad moments, some occurring even before the working day had begun. One morning I arrived at work to be greeted with the sight of a chap being wrestled to the floor. I happened to recognise the police-man who was doing the apprehending. He stopped mid-scuffle, turned to me and, in a bright voice, proffered, 'Oh, hi Rach!'

'Erm, oh, hi Dave.'

After this briefest of exchanges, he resumed the brawl to cuff the guy, murmuring, 'You're nicked!' and I continued on upstairs to our office. The criminal, who was well known, had been caught stealing from handbags upstairs and had been forging stolen prescriptions.

'Whose bags had he been rifling?' I queried.

'One of the secretaries, I gather,' replied a colleague. 'He'd nicked her purse. She got it back, though.'

Illicit trading in prescriptions can be a problem. I became worried about another mum when it became apparent that she was selling her prescriptions for tranquilisers, antidepressants and painkillers, telling the GP she had lost them or left the medication at a friend's house, that sort of thing. The GP had no idea of her history (which was worrying in a drug-related way) as she was new to the surgery.

Sometimes, this sort of information comes through to us before it reaches other professionals – in this case, the woman's previous health visitor in another part of the country had called me to advise of her concerns. As health visitors, we always record our information, and this is often shared between the GP and other health visitors (if consent is gained) as the situation unfolds, but in this case the GP was busy, overwhelmed even, and was doling out the meds until I read of the frequency of the woman's visits and requests and alerted the GP to what she was up to. She had been able to get repeat prescriptions via a telephone request; now that this was stopped she would have to come in and see said GP to be reassessed each time she made a request.

I was visiting her at this time and she put two and two together and got angry with me, as I had interrupted her little side line. Social care became involved as it transpired that police had given them some intel regarding dealers coming in to the area. This woman was quite possibly being used as a dealer herself by the 'county lines' dealers.

The social worker and I visited together; we were concerned about the safety not only of mum in this instance, but of the toddler who was also resident in this house. Who else was visiting? Was this a 'cuckooing' situation, possibly? This is where a violent and aggressive drug dealer takes over a property, using it to facilitate the buying and selling of drugs. Often the real tenant or owner of the property is threatened with a beating if they don't comply. When the dealer has finished using the home, they cut off the telephone line and electricity after savage violence, so that the victim cannot call for help and is left without any means of heat or light.

We were advised not to go alone. So on my final visit to the house I decided to wait until the social worker arrived. In the meantime, the client in question rocked up with her daughter and a gaggle of friends. She said she was ill with a migraine, and could I come back another day? The social worker arrived at this point and a difficult conversation ensued, during which her friends crowded around us – a little too close for comfort – and told us to fuck off (a common phrase in my professional life).

Despite the antagonism, we made it clear that we were extremely concerned for her daughter's safety. Several neighbours had reported that they had been threatened by a male in the house, and this had been relayed to the police and social care. The very next day the child was removed by social workers, as they were concerned in the extreme about this child's safety and the mother's ability to protect her child.

* * *

So much of the job of being a health visitor is about responding to very difficult situations and trying to help people who may not actually want you there. Sometimes our interventions mean a family is able to stay together, and sometimes there is nothing we can really do. On occasion though, my job allows me to be more proactive and set up a resource that I think – based on what I have seen out in the community – could really help my clients. It's always a joy to be asked to come up with a new initiative, and co-ordinate with all the relevant parties to try to make it happen.

I had been seconded to a 'Building Community Capacity' course and tasked with thinking of something to benefit my neighbourhood, that could be implemented by moi. It had to be researched, evidenced, referenced – in other words, I had to be able to prove that it was both needed and achievable.

A few weeks earlier, the local food bank had contacted me to tell me how little storage space they had for baby items such as nappies, wipes, etc. So, I thought, what about if I set up a nappy bank? I knew there was room at the Children's Centre – these are government-funded centres specifically for the use and benefit of parents and their babies and children. It's where parenting courses are held, as well as health visitor clinics, parent and baby groups, baby singing groups, etc – all things to enable families to socialise and learn or just have fun. So I just need to work out who to chat up for funding. There were a couple of banks (of the financial kind this time) in the area who might wish to be known for something other than being one of 'those bastard banks' after the major recession. Perhaps one of them would help?

I established who the communities funding manager was and sent through a missive. He replied, asking for a more detailed proposal. I returned one and waited for the reply. I also wondered if we could supply toothpastes and brushes for both parents and babies, in view of NHS dental care being in short supply. Oh, and what about tampons and pads for us gals – sometimes, when skint, we women look at the remaining fiver in our purse and have to toss up whether it's baked potatoes tonight so we can purchase the super plus, or whether to just ferret around and hopefully find some old forgotten Tampax with the wrapping still intact, ideally in a toiletry bag, handbag or coat pocket.

I wondered about how clients would fulfil the criteria for help from the nappy bank – I would have to think about the circumstances that would lead you to request such help and devise an eligibility form. OK, so unemployment, redundancy, low income, debt, an unexpected crisis – I would have to do some profiling to assess who was actually asking and why. The form would have to include the client's details, how many children were in the family, and what age group, in order to assess the sizing of nappies – i.e. new-borns or pull-ups for toddlers. Also if extras were needed – such as the toothbrushes and pastes and the sanitary products. There could be limitations – say, no more than three applications in three months.

I heard back from the communities officer at the bank who said that my proposal had been discussed at their allocations meeting and I had successfully secured £1,000 for the start up. Brilliant.

We had our photo taken for a piece for the *Bournemouth Echo* – my health visitor student at the time, a staff member from the local nursery, the man from the bank, my manager and me – and we duly grinned and gurned alongside the nappies, toothpastes and tampons. On publication, the first thing I did was turn to the comments at the foot of the online piece. It's always so entertaining. Wow. How do people get so sad? There were comments such as:

'I made my finances work when I had my children, it's about time this lot did – expect they spend their money on drugs.'

Or:

'What next – when we run out of wine, will there be a wine bank for these feckless families?'

I guess these commenters just don't know the amount of poverty out there and perhaps they don't care, preferring to make uneducated (and misspelt) judgements about other people's lives of which they know nothing.

So, the cheque was paid into the local authority who managed the fund, the Children's Centre stored the supplies, and the workers allocated them when a referral form was presented. Various professionals could refer to the nappy bank: health visitors in the vicinity, GPs and social workers, directing those in need to the centre.

There are often occasions that income unexpectedly does not come in and bills unexpectedly go out. I know all about that. That and the grinding reality of trying to make sense of zero-hour contracts, debt and unpreparedness for costs such as children's coats, shoes, school trips, car trouble. It was often overwhelming, but at least we could help, albeit in a small way.

I left the area some years ago but gather that some version of the nappy bank still runs, funded by public donations. I still get emails and signpost them accordingly to the Children's Centre that houses it.

Around this time, a colleague withdrew from her role as health visitor at the refuge in the town centre and I decided to step up and fill the gap. With a bit of clever juggling I reckoned I could fit it in. I was working full-time as a health visitor at a surgery about a mile away and I wanted to help out. I offered, as no one else had, and I was good to go.

Refuges are for families fleeing domestic abuse. They are largely underfunded by the government, with limited capacity, hence the increasingly few places to be had. There were women here who had been stabbed and beaten. The statistics say that, on average, women suffer 50 incidents of abuse before asking for help.

Then there is coercive control, which is also a crime, and involves belittling and criticising in order to erode confidence and assume power over someone. It's subtler than outright violence, but no less effective in destroying the victim's sense of worth and breaking their spirit. It can encompass rewarding and punishing – keeping their victim on the back foot by being nice one day and punishing them the next. Where are you going? Who with? The perpetrator often disguises it as love or affection: 'I want to help you choose your clothes' ('Not too revealing – you don't want to look like a tart'). They may insist on shared emails and phone contract to allow them constant monitoring.

I found my way to the refuge building – no easy task, as the location is of course a secret – and was shown around. Each room had a living area, a kitchenette and one bedroom – no matter how many children a resident had.

The folk in the office were welcoming. I was surprised that there was a male manager; I wasn't expecting that. The rest were women. All were key workers, skilled at advocacy, claiming benefits, dealing with the housing department and sourcing school places – there was an atmosphere of experienced calm from those who had lived life and wanted to share their wisdom.

The health visitor role was to assist with all of those things, but also to directly assess health needs for both the parent and the babies and children. Did they need check-ups? A six-week contact with a GP if they had just fled with a newborn? Did older children need development checks to identify problems with vision, hearing, speech, behaviour, mental health issues, sleep problems, outstanding immunisations?

Sometimes all of those factors were in play. I would make the required referrals and then often find that, by the time the appointment had come through, the family had moved on because the perpetrator had discovered their location. It was frustrating to know that they could have had help with lots of health issues, but the frequent moves inhibited that. The move to a refuge, often without any warning, was confusing, even if it did ensure their safety.

Some women needed help finding school places for their children, or help with claiming benefits, which would take up to six or even eight weeks to come through. They depended upon food bank vouchers until then.

Sometimes the women would leave after a short while, returning to the family home and back to the violence. Life without the usual, familiar things could feel daunting – the children would say that they missed their bedrooms and friends and so back they would go. The police are now much better at dealing with and prosecuting offenders, but it's still a slow and laborious process.

Occasionally, a resident would go out for an extended period and another would tell us that they were meeting the perpetrator, which cancelled out any benefit in being there – it also prevented someone else from having a much-needed refuge place.

The locations of refuges are unidentified until there is a place secured for you. At that point, a social worker or a health visitor – I have done this – takes you and deposits you safely there. If it's the middle of the night, you're accompanied by the out-of-hours social worker. You may have arrived with your children but no clothes, no familiar things, no money and what feels like very little dignity. Some arrive without tampons or sanitary towels when having a period.

Many of the families were damaged and children would often have behavioural difficulties that Child and Adolescent Mental Health Service (CAHMS) would say were not address-able until the family had found a period of stability and calm. But what if they didn't ever find that? Surely it's better to offer the parent some kind of therapeutic intervention at the time to perhaps ease the situation as much as possible?

Often there are physical problems to try to deal with, too. Children may have squints or speech and hearing problems, or they might be receiving treatment or waiting for operations or medical care where they were living, and so then it's a case of starting all over again, waiting for said intervention at a new address.

I would let the workers and the clients know when I would be visiting, so residents would know I was available if they needed help with health issues, or any issues really. Sometimes I would knock on their doors to ensure that they knew I was there if they had forgotten. Occasionally, I would be invited in to discuss their worries. They were so down in that deep well of despair that sometimes it felt they were almost unreachable. It was only the arrival of several black bags full of second-hand clothing that could incentivise them to leave their rooms where, in the centre of the communal area, the girls would be lightening quick to choose the best of the donation – a new dress or top – and then back to their room.

The GP surgery was close by for the next script of fluoxetine – an anti-depressant. The food bank was a bus ride away. The shops were within walking distance.

After a few months, residents got to move on to a flat, still under the auspices of the refuge – there were five available – to enable them to get back out in civvy street. First they had to do the requisite work of the Pattern Changing Programme or Freedom Project – both courses that unpack the behaviours of perpetrators to help the victim understand the *modus operandi* of previous partners, or sometimes even parents, who had abused them, in an attempt to avoid the same, repeated set of behaviours which had led to their admission to a refuge.

The apartments ran like any other rental, but with access to the staff and support as and when required. Six months was the optimum time to be spent there, but often it overran due to lack of available and affordable housing to move to.

Residents of the hostel included senior professional women, working-class women and stay-at-home mums.

Whilst working as health visitor to the refuge, I managed to extract some money from a nearby bank (the same one that had helped to set up the nappy bank) to fund, in a small way, some extra supplies for those fleeing domestic violence, to augment their welcome packs. There was tea and coffee provided in the pack, but sadly no milk! So we arranged for a carton of UHT milk to be added to the supplies. I believe, at that point, there were no tampons or sanitary towels issued so, again, these were essential items to be included. We also included a 'treat' – for instance, a bar of chocolate. Something small but thoughtful, as treats were in very short supply.

I believe that the £500 donated only lasted for six months, after which the welcome pack became sadly depleted again.

* * *

Throughout this book, I've wanted to convey the very best bits of my job as well as some of the challenges. But there is one area of our work that affects us all profoundly. Very rarely, we have to deal with the heartbreak of sudden infant death syndrome (SIDS).

We advise parents about safe sleeping on all new birth visits, especially the risks of falling asleep on a sofa or a chair and advice about co-sleeping – when it's unsafe to do so, for instance, if you are exhausted you can fall into a deep sleep; if there are pillows and quilts and gaps between the headboard and bed; if you have been drinking excessive alcohol or taking substances. Health visitors outline all of these things and work out, with you, what is safe and what isn't, and ask to see the baby's sleeping arrangements.

Rarely, though, no amount of advice can prevent this most tragic of events occurring. One morning, I visited a young single mother called Tracey who, in her extreme exhaustion, had fallen asleep on a sofa with her baby, who was five months old. Tracey had woken to find her precious baby cold, lifeless next to her. The GP had been called and all the attendant processes were underway. She was ashen and hollowed-eyed, having visibly aged about 10 years overnight, and repeatedly going over the events leading up to this catastrophe.

In my career to date, I have met three women and their families who have experienced SIDS. They are each and every one – and there was a total of 1,360 such deaths in 2017 – tragedies of unfathomable proportions. Families are rendered fractured and reeling by the magnitude of such baffling events. One enters their homes feeling beyond miserable and totally inadequate. Words, good intentions and love are useless and neutralised by the horror and injustice of it all.

As health visitors, we are more than aware that we can only hopelessly offer our enduring support and practical advice about registering the death. We can only really look on while families await with despair the outcome of the grim post-mortem, which often clarifies nothing, especially when, as in this case, there are no conclusive findings beyond the possibility of a viral illness, which can occur with any and all babies and children.

The guilt is overwhelming for all concerned – should we have noticed something? Were there signs that were missed? Was she sleepier than usual? Unsettled? Why didn't I notice something? Should I have taken her to the GP? The self-loathing and endless blame feel like a leaden cloak to be worn in perpetuity. A thousand million question marks. The baby's things, the emptiness of the shiny cot and new mattress, the freshly purchased baby grows, the jolly toys and the deep well of hopeless silence – all exacerbate the torture.

Our visits can appear to be insensitive: 'You only visit when there is a baby, don't you? Well, there isn't one. Why have you come?' The anger can be directed at all comers. The confusion and overwhelming fog reigns and engulfs, like your own personal cloud of misery and despondency with no accurate forecast as to when it will depart. Like all loss and grief, there are the various stages to be endured – denial, anger, bargaining, depression and acceptance – in any order and for any length of time, but the health visitor can and will be there to walk with you.

Among the practical support we can offer is signposting you to other professionals for support. For example, the Lullaby Trust, which is a charity devoted to support and information for parents, which is very much needed at such a time, as well as the GP and counselling – either individual or group. And we can even help when you start to think about the possibility of more children. When the time is right.

This is a real leap of faith for many, of course. Being vulnerable again. The Care of the Next Infant service (CONI) involves a health professional, usually a health visitor, who can give you extra support when you start to think about having another child, and after the birth. We can offer regular home visits, so new parents can talk freely about any worries, seek advice and borrow movement monitors which pick up movements as the baby breathes and will ring an alarm if movements stop for longer than 20 seconds. There is training on basic life support and keeping a symptom diary to record the baby's health. A 'Baby Check' booklet or app can help understandably nervous parents decide whether to seek medical help for their baby.

There are weekly visits from us, ideally on the same day of the week and with the same weighing scales to plot baby's growth on a huge and detailed weight chart to detect any weight loss. We can provide a room thermometer and guidance on bedding and clothing. For instance, as with all new babies, there are to be no pillows or quilts until two years of age. And despite the temptation of affixing cot bumpers to the cot sides, these are a 'no-no' too.

As is often the case, Tracey was very quickly expecting again. She had benefited from a spell of counselling and had also given up smoking – a big risk factor. We advised about taking folic acid and regular midwife and consultant ante-natal appointments. She had done brilliantly. She was happy, but cautiously so; there were of course mixed emotions, but the pregnancy progressed relatively uneventfully. Tracey had a lovely baby girl, by way of a normal delivery. All went smoothly and Tracey and baby Lisa went home.

However, accompanying the cards and flowers was an attendant sense of trepidation. The lovely midwife visited every day for 10 days and then I took over Tracey and Lisa's care thereafter. We usually weighed Lisa on the same scales and at the same time each week, plotting it on an enormous gridded Sheffield chart for ease of interpretation. If there was a dip, there was a corresponding dip in Tracey's nerve and confidence, and I would make an appointment with the GP to get Lisa checked out.

Tracey wanted the service, but some previously bereaved parents don't. It's totally voluntary. However, Tracey didn't want the movement monitor after trying it for a short time. It would go off when her new baby was fine and dandy so it became a sort of anti-reassurance and was consequently abandoned.

Once we had gone past the five-month point – the time of her previous devastating loss – Tracey began to believe in her competence and gained that confidence that had eluded her. With each passing day, she relaxed a little more. Night times were always anxiety-inducing, but even they were getting more bearable.

After six months, I asked if Tracey wanted to continue. She hesitated and said that she would give it a go, but could we talk about weaning before giving up the weekly sessions? Could she still call if worried? Of course. Often parents in these situations also have rapid access to the paediatric ward if required. So my final visit to Tracey's home was to discuss weaning for Lisa. This was something that made her anxious – she just needed some pointers about how to approach the process, like most mums do.

Weaning – getting babies onto solid foods – can be a scary process. In the past, new parents were offered advice at home at the four-month mark, with a view to starting at around six months. The discussion revolved around types of food, textures, how often, how to recognise when the baby is ready, baby-led or purees, or both, and what not to offer. This allowed us to advise on what can be a fraught process and is the beginning of a child's relationship with food. But there is no four-month visit any more. We would see mums at clinic though, if they attended, for a short discussion on this topic.

The obesity crisis tells us that, perhaps, this should be reinstated as a matter of urgency – after all, it allows us to positively influence the whole family's attitude to food, so surely, this is a wasted public health opportunity?

Instead, some health visitors organise group weaning demonstrations either in a clinic setting or, alternatively, in a client's lovely kitchen when they are willing to open up their home to other mums. These are the best fun – getting to simmer, bake, roast veg and blitz them up to a puree whilst chatting about the equipment required: plastic spoons, bowls, bibs, the hand blender, the plastic sheet to place under the high chair (essential if you are partial to pristine floors, as babies will chuck their newly discovered food around with abandon and wear it as a jaunty, if adhesive, accessory). I tend to suggest making your own food, because you get to know what's in it and you can be so much more adventurous. Jars and pre-made stuff are OK, although today, as I write, there is a recall for a certain brand with a concern of 'tampering'.

Nothing beats homemade, nutritious, seasonal stuff made with love, and it's cheaper to boot. You can just cook what the family is eating, without the addition of salt or sugar. No need for rusks or baby rice. You can oven bake some dainty wholemeal bread slices for a teething stick, instead of shop-bought. Baby rice is like wallpaper paste. Have you tried it?

It's about enjoying food and encouraging the ritual of sharing at an early age. Too many mums don't sit down to eat with their babies – most haven't got the time and many parents, understandably, eat later when baby has gone to bed. But, consequently, children are growing up having never experienced anyone sitting down to eat with them. When it is pointed out, it seems obvious.

Of course, it doesn't help that lots of new-build housing is not designed to accommodate a family dining table any more, meaning that the opportunity for socialisation and joyful family chatter at meal times is, sadly, denied. We really ought to be more French in our 'foodie' outlook. The 24/7 nature of our working lives erodes the integrity of a family gathering together. It's time to reclaim the lunch break, methinks. Let's make it an hour, at least. If we were in Carcassonne, or somewhere equally gloriously idyllic *en France*, we would be looking at at least two hours.

It was fairly commonplace in my early days of health visiting that dad would come home from work to have lunch with his family. It's rare to the point of extinction now and we are, possibly, diminished for all that.

Chapter Ten
Toast

Some years back I did the extra one-year training course so I could become a practice teacher. This means that – like my field work teacher, Jan, back in Mutley Plain in Plymouth – I have trained five students to become health visitors. The current health visitor course, as laid out by our registering body the Nursing and Midwifery Council (NMC), entails some weeks out in the field with someone like me and some weeks at studying at uni. I have enjoyed sharing the love whilst we worked and learned together in our quest for the best outcomes for our mums.

Of course, the reality often bites early, and some are put off the whole concept of health visiting altogether when they encounter some of the most squalid and neglected homes imaginable. One student decided it was not for her when she sat in one such house – there were soiled nappies, dog shit, empty cans, takeaway leftovers and both clean and dirty washing all entangled in piles on the floor and on furniture. I could see that the student was horrified. She still asked some of the subtler questions such as, 'How are you coping with your housework?' and 'Is there anything that is impacting your ability to cope at the moment?' The reply to the first question was, 'Yeah, coping with the housework, thanks,' but the second reply was, 'We've just had a bereavement and so I am a bit all over the place…'

Either way, chaos reigned and so we initiated a discussion about emotions surrounding loss – denial, anger, depression, acceptance and the cycle which has to be undergone. We walked out of the house (I had a sandwich stuck to my shoe; on closer inspection, it turned out to be coronation chicken) with plans to return in a week to see if things were the same. Bearing in mind there were two under-fives who had the right to live in a safe home environment. It's always a balance, isn't it? Life isn't always perfect and sometimes you have to give someone a bit of slack, but if things don't improve then there has to be a bit more intervention and guidance.

I took another student to visit a family due to one of the children having drunk from a Calpol bottle – an unquantifiable amount, but probably quite small. Darren, aged two, was rushed to A&E, but remained well. We went some days later to assess the home situation and make suggestions about how to avoid similar situations in future. Most people have worked it out for themselves, but some might need prompting.

On approaching the front door, we observed a loo seat leaned up against the wall with a small nugget of shite adjacent to it. Today Darren was eating scraps of toast from the grubby floor inside. I suggested to his mother, Margaret, that Darren be made some fresh toast, as he appeared to be hungry. We made attempts to engage him with a book from my bag; he cried, as Mum had flounced off into the kitchen, clearly unhappy at my direction. She returned huffily with a piece of the white sliced, dripping in butter, and Darren's eyes lit up. She proceeded to place it directly on what looked like a swish new red sofa. No plate. No seating for Darren. The £1,000 sofa (free for the first year, 36 instalments thereafter, no doubt) was his plate.

After some chit-chat about home safety – where were the medicines kept? In a locked or high cupboard? – the thought swirled in my head and that of my student that perhaps this was an opportunity to bring in some discussion around table manners, or at least how to not ruin a piece of furniture that could last for 10 years, but looked likely to last 10 minutes in this case.

My lovely bright-eyed student Debbie suggested that perhaps she could fetch a plate for Darren? She got up to demonstrate that she was, indeed, willing to do so, but

Margaret had had enough: 'Right, you two, I've had it. Fuck off out of here if you're going to lecture me.' Opening the front door, she meant it. 'Go on! Fuck off.'

I said quietly that perhaps we could arrange another time more suitable for her. But as we walked through the exit, the door was slammed shut behind us with a great thwack, metaphorically hitting us on the backsides. That was the first visit of the day.

Next day, we had a phone call from the headteacher at the local first school, saying they had just had a visit from a two-year-old child in a sleep suit and full nappy who was eyeing up the contents of the lunchboxes in the corridor. She was helping herself to the pick of the best, and no one had any idea who she was. Could I help at all?

We trotted up to the school entrance, were buzzed in and there she was, in the school office with the secretaries, looking pretty pleased with herself. Mum was on her way, as someone had worked out who she was and the family lived close to the school. Mum, Isobel, arrived looking dishevelled and embarrassed. I immediately recognised her, as she had recently had a new baby, her second child. I said that I would call her, if that was OK. Isobel quickly removed her toddler from the premises after a brief chat with the head about how she got there. Mum muttered something about her lively toddler being very adventurous, and apologised profusely.

Toast

I called her later as promised. Isobel was tearful – she had become depressed, overwhelmed with the arrival of a second child, and had fallen asleep due to exhaustion. Lily had escaped through the unlocked front door.

'Can you visit?' she asked me.

'Yes, absolutely. Could I bring my student, Debbie, too?'

'Yes, please do.'

People often say, 'Oh your second child is easy,' but it's frequently far from that. The two children have differing and competing needs. One requires you to be clamped to the sofa, feeding all day, while the older child demands to be taken swimming or to the park – the very last place you wish to be – making you feel consumed with guilt.

The first child shocks us with their newness and our naïve obliviousness to the magnitude of what lies ahead. The second child knocks us into another dimension of anxiety and fretting about the impact on our first child. Have I made them feel unloved and abandoned? Isolated and racked with guilt, we faux smile and navigate life and the other parents who can, sometimes, let's face it, be quite 'judgey'.

Isobel told us that the only time she felt happy was when she was in the car alone, when no one could make any demands of her. She felt as though she had abandoned her first child, and felt inadequate and isolated. Her husband was working long hours and was exhausted when he arrived at home. She was missing the companionship of work and her partner's support through the day. She was barely sleeping and there wasn't any family support nearby.

Extended family support is a big issue, because those new parents who have someone to pop in on them, or offer a night's babysitting, who they can ask, 'Would you look after them whilst I go to the hairdresser? The dentist? The cinema? Yoga?' are light years ahead of those who have nobody to help them and no one with whom to share the experience and care, even just occasionally. It can be a very isolating experience with no one to love and nurture you as a new mum.

Other cultures often have a more supportive and sociable time. Parents, grandparents and friends come to do the cooking or cleaning and ensure everyone gets fed. Certainly my time in Hackney and Tower Hamlets demonstrated that our British culture, especially the working-class culture (unless mum lived a few doors away in the same neighbourhood), is one of, 'You've made your bed, now lie in it.' Often it was a case of 'You're on your own now.'

With the Uppers, the grandparents, especially, involve themselves in the lives of their grandchildren because they view their progeny as the future and invest accordingly in new baby and mother, by way of putting the baby's name down for a posh school. Or the grandparents might move in to cook, clean, iron and feed the whole bally lot. Or they might offer to pay for a night-time maternity nurse, allowing the new parents some sanity-enhancing sleep. Or perhaps a nanny.

In this instance, Isobel didn't have anyone coming around to help her out when her husband was at work, and it seemed to be taking its toll. When there are numerous and significant factors going wrong in a family, one of the first things to consider is mental health – and depression in particular. We use numerous approaches and tools to establish how best to help and/or come to a diagnosis and, in doing so, find a way forward.

One example of a diagnostic tool often used by health visitors is the Whooley questions: during the past month, have you felt bothered by feeling down, depressed or hopeless? During the past month have you been bothered by little interest or pleasure in doing things? Then there are other scoring systems, such as the GAD-7, a questionnaire aimed at diagnosing general anxiety disorder, and PHQ-9, which is used by GPs, health visitors and mental health professionals to help diagnose depression. We tend to use a combination of all of these. Helpfully, we have often seen the mum in the antenatal period, so will remember how things were then and can compare assessments to have a clear view on what is happening now.

We carry these questions, or variants of them, in our heads but, in reality, they are difficult questions to ask.

Some clients will be reserved and want to offer as little as possible because they may feel that we are out to judge, which, believe it or not, we are not – we're there to put support in place if it's needed.

On the other hand, some clients will gladly open up and be relieved that you asked. You have to try asking these questions as evenly as you can, giving the impression that you do not fear any answer; then your client will hopefully understand that not only are you taking her thoughts and feelings seriously, but you'll offer the necessary advice and support in the same spirit – transparently and with integrity.

When I put the questions to Isobel she had a high score. I suggested seeing the GP and offered regular listening visits until such time that she felt they were not needed. Listening visits are where we offer to see a mum, usually weekly, to give her the opportunity to offload. It's often as simple as listening to her and echoing the sentiments back, in order to demonstrate that we have understood her worries, allowing her to perhaps reflect or make a decision or observation as she continues.

We managed to help find some childcare for two-year-old Lily to lighten the load, and hopefully prevent any more solo adventures. We also involved a very lovely community nurse who could offer some ongoing sleep work for Isobel and both of her children, which helped enormously. Once a family starts benefitting from our intervention we can usually reduce our visits. Happily, in this instance, after a series of visits, Isobel gained in confidence and was able to continue in her own style with self-belief, safe in the knowledge that she could come back to us at any point, either by phone, or clinic attendance, to ask for further support if required.

Post-natal depression strikes more commonly than we think, and it can be a fickle beast. All new parents are sleep-deprived, but there is a certain dark-ringed, hollow-eyed look that I recognise. The experience of having a baby often involves a heady mixture of fear, elation and exhaustion, with a hefty measure of anxiety thrown in. But we also may question our identity all the time. Is this my life now? Having battled to the pinnacle of my chosen profession, in whatever field that is, am I now reduced to the emptying of the dishwasher as the highlight of the day?

Sometimes we just want to be somewhere else. Or somebody else.

Health visitors can organise a referral for counselling, or you can refer yourself. Have you spoken to your GP? Shall I visit you weekly for a while to listen to how you feel about what's worrying you? Sometimes we have to ask about feelings of self-harm or, indeed, is anyone else harming you?

Listening is what I do. That and asking a few pertinent questions, of course. With every answer, observation, professional intuition, I have to decipher if you are OK. A flicker in your eyes, an inadvertent touch of your nose, an unwitting shifting of your lower limbs... I have to try to understand what is really going on and what the risks might be if I walk out of your door and leave you with an insurmountable problem that I did not pick up on.

It could end badly for both of us.

Chapter Eleven
Kindness as a Political Act

Today, I am visiting a woman called Lucy who is pregnant but living in a homeless hostel. The hostel rules do not allow for a baby, so mum-to-be needs to be rehoused. The baby is due in July, and so there is an urgency about this as we are at the end of June. There is no family, no money; she claims a little over £200 per month in benefits to cover everything. Around £50 is for rent.

Lucy has just been discharged from hospital. There having been some concerns regarding the baby's growth, the placenta and also Lucy's high blood pressure. She'll have regular scans going forward, but if the baby looks like she is not growing, and certainly if Lucy's blood pressure remains high, they will undertake a lower segmental caesarean section (LSCS), as the placenta will not be functioning efficiently and there will be risks to Lucy, too.

Lucy is guarded. She has had a difficult childhood and her parents were emotionally and physically abusive – she only stays in touch with her mother. There are no other family members. I have applied to a charity for a cot, which I do for quite a few mums who are in need, and it has been approved. She does not have any kind of advocate or support. If she had been in care, like some of the residents have, she would have been eligible for a financial package on moving out into her allocated home, but she was not. She is on her own.

She engages very little with health professionals. Being very suspicious, she keeps me at arm's length. She talks tough despite her angelic appearance – all long blonde curls and baby blue 'peepers' – but under the veneer is a very frightened girl who doesn't really understand why I am kind to her. I sense that, despite her best efforts not to, she quite likes me. I am seemingly the only health professional that keeps her appointments and sees her on her own turf. The midwives have phoned to say that they feel threatened by her, and would I visit with them jointly? My response was, if you treat her kindly, she is absolutely fine and you'll be fine too.

A social worker turns up at the same time as me. We are ushered into the reception waiting room. It's full of grubby plastic furniture, a pool table, some dead pot plants and a noticeboard with some photos of long-forgotten residents who appeared to be happy in a fleeting moment. There are handwritten notes sellotaped to the wall advertising jobs at

McDonald's and other various apprenticeships: 'Apply to Kevin for further details. £8 per hour.' The kitchen is adjacent to the reception and people come and go but lock each door every time they leave. A local supermarket drops off the day's bread and baking each night for the residents.

We sit in the drab and inhospitable room waiting for Lucy to show up – they buzzed her and she is getting dressed. The social worker is exhausted from the stress of her caseload and has been in court all the previous day. Most of her clients hate her and are not shy about telling her – taking their kids away isn't a vote-winner. She tells me that she could probably earn as much working in Lidl, despite being responsible for 20 highly-vulnerable families with complexity and abuse as standard. I tell her that I have just seen a family that morning where the mother of a child had been living in a car for some time before she had been rehoused – and before the birth of her child. We both cried. What a shitty life this is for some.

We compose ourselves before Lucy comes in with a cup-a-soup in hand that she has 'borrowed' from another resident. She says she had nothing to eat and no money until the 25th of the month. It is now the 4th. She generally lives off ready meals from Iceland and looks pale and wan – she had a Twirl for breakfast today. So the social worker emails the food bank for food for the week. I manage to extract some cash from the emergency budget for her. I also have £20 in my purse and so I offer it to her. She is taken aback but eventually accepts it. She needs help in an immediate sense. I ask if there is anyone else who could help her financially. 'Nope,' is the reply. I make an appointment to see her the following week, knowing that she will be in exactly the same situation then. So we have to go back to see that she's OK, and again put in place the food bank referral and anything else that arises. How can we walk away?

Lucy had her baby by emergency section due to foetal distress. She had a friend who was her birthing partner. She got rehoused in Poole, eventually, but found it pretty isolating there, I gather. I get the occasional text from her to say that she and her daughter, Holly, are doing well and thanking me for my help.

It's tough without family close by. It's tougher when they are totally absent.

* * *

We health visitors now work 'corporately'. No tailored, individual visiting pattern according to your need. We are 'commissioned' for five meetings, known as episodes: an antenatal contact, a new birth contact, a six-week contact, a 10-12 month developmental contact and a two-year contact.

Families in Wales are in receipt of nine universal contacts; in Northern Ireland they are commissioned for seven but are increasing to nine. In Scotland, health visitors are commissioned for 11 universal contacts. The service no longer feels like a service, and more like a series of siloed functions. No one consistent professional necessarily sees you – it can be a series of different health visitors.

The Health and Social Care Act of 2012 shifted responsibility for health visiting services to local government from the NHS in England, along with other public health provision, from October 2015. The funding that the NHS had received to pay for this was transferred to local councils, but it wasn't ring-fenced. This meant that, in practice, the service was the victim of the cost-saving measures that local councils have made across the board, leading to a reduction in practising health visitors.

But health visitors are the only nurses who have, as their main focus, prevention of ill-health and promotion of well-being. These qualified professionals – who have also studied an extra year on top of their nursing or midwifery qualification – have unique access to families through home visiting, which enables us to identify health needs early, and often before they become critical, wreaking irreparable damage.

There is currently, at my surgery, a three-week wait to see a GP, a 12-week waiting list for a family support worker, also for speech and language therapy, a *year*-long waiting list for an assessment for autism, and a 10-year wait for a local authority home. Usually, applicants are advised that they will never get a place at all.

Food-bank usage has never been as high. Self-harm and associated mental health conditions are at alarming levels.

The rate of SIDS – sudden infant death syndrome – is rising again after a sustained period of decline. Childhood obesity is a real and debilitating issue. Both of these problems are associated with poverty and deprivation.

Effective primary care is based on trusting relationships between practitioners and patients, as well as between the healthcare professionals providing that care. With fewer of us health visitors to go around, maintaining and building those relationships becomes more difficult. Just when there is an overwhelming imperative to focus on prevention and self-care, these services are being cut. I think that *all* our visits are based on trust. From sorting out the redecoration of a neglected flat for an isolated Bangladeshi mum in Limehouse, to working with those survivors of domestic abuse in a refuge, to allowing clients to call you out of hours on days off and on your own mobile.

The rigid framework that we work within is a barrier to people accessing our services when they need them. If we are unaware of someone's post-natal depression because we haven't seen that mum for ages, how can we possibly put in place any talking therapies, any listening visits, any recommendation to see her GP (and hitherto we would have talked to the GP to make him or her aware of our concerns, or that someone was heading their way – that is much harder to do now) or for a family outreach worker for extra support? If I don't know what the client is thinking or feeling because I don't have the opportunity to talk to them and understand the family's needs any more, how can I help them?

All over the country, families are descending into a spiral of chaos without a health visitor to engage with at the start of whatever the issue might be. Things that could have been averted or de-escalated, or smoothed out earlier, are now turning into full-blown crises.

The end result is that we are a crisis-driven service rather than the professionals who dealt in that sweet, old-fashioned concept of prevention – which is what we have always been, since the beginnings of the service over 150 years ago.

Historically, we have operated on the medical model of working, meaning that, among other things, we worked closely with GPs, basing ourselves in their surgeries. This had been in place since the mid-1970s, but is now giving way to the public health model. This means – admirably – focusing on specific areas of health such as parenthood and early weeks, maternal mental health, breastfeeding, preventing minor illnesses and accidents, reducing hospital admissions, the two-year check to include transfer to school, and readiness to learn support. It means we are based in a community hub or somewhere similar.

However, the cutting of ties with GPs means that, while we still liaise with them and they with us, it's more likely to be via an email now or a 'task' sent using the software system specific to our area. In the past, we would have had a multi-disciplinary meeting on a Friday, sharing a lunch. Here we could compare notes; a GP could suggest a visit to a family as they might not have been seen in their home situation – maybe they were new to the surgery, for instance – or the GP could ask us if we have any concerns about a patient they had recently seen. This meant that the flow of information and questioning went both ways. Meetings do sometimes happen, but we are increasingly separate and remote from GPs.

Whenever there's a serious case review, which happens when a child is seriously injured or worse, the safeguarding board who are responsible for the review always, almost without exception, conclude that communication between professionals should have, and could have, been improved upon. They identify several opportunities and occasions where more communication should have taken place.

We hear, unofficially, that as health visitors retire, they might be replaced with a cheaper alternative – those less skilled, with less training, yet who will no doubt have to oversee even more troubled families. They might well be quite quickly overwhelmed, making it even more stressful and harder to make a difference. The turnover rate of these professionals joining and then leaving the profession will doubtless be rapid, and so too will the dilution and fragmentation, meaning the ultimate disintegration of the once-valued role of health visiting could well be complete. Let's hope this unofficial prediction does not come true.

*   *   *

Today, I am acting as duty health visitor. This means that I process data. Specifically, I interpret each accident and emergency (A&E) or minor injuries unit (MIU) attendance notification that comes through via email to the health visiting team. Then enter the salient detail into the relevant section of the child's records.

Babies and children are taken to A&E for all sorts of reasons. Sometimes for illnesses such as colds, diarrhoea, vomiting, high temperature, a rash. Or perhaps a foreign body stuck up the right nostril, they swallowed a coin or were bitten by a dog. The baby might be grizzly, have sunburn, not be feeding, not weeing, not pooing. Or maybe the child ate some of grandma's meds (always keep the meds in a locked cupboard and get grandma to do the same) or chewed a Persil tab (pop these up and out of the way too). There are many entries in the records that read, 'Child visited Minor Injuries Unit with a viral illness. No further action at this point.' Everything is recorded.

On this particular morning I have over 80 of these to process. It takes all morning, from 10am until 1pm. Meanwhile, I am also trying to field phone calls from mums who want to run a concern past us – sometimes a minor health issue, or perhaps the washing machine has broken, can we help?

While I am tapping away at the keyboard, the community midwives come to discuss the antenatal ladies who are due later in the year and the ongoing issues that they present: one woman is an ex-intravenous drug user and is with a much older, controlling man; another has had two previous children removed and is now with a new partner – we will have to see how she parents this baby due at Christmas.

I also have a stack of PPNs to process. These are public protection notices. Essentially, this is where the police share their data about domestic abuse incidents with social workers, health visitors and school nurses, and again we enter a summary of the information onto the relevant child's records. It comes in via email but it will be a in scanned, written format so it's hard to decipher – did someone 'thaw' a phone at Miss X? Oh, no, he threw it, of course.

This information really is of utmost importance, and is certainly relevant to our interventions and thought processes. We will often need to contact these families to let them know that we are in possession of this sensitive information, and could we possibly pop round to discuss how you are a) protecting yourself and b) protecting the children? If the answer to either or both is c) not so much, then what are the barriers? And can we help to remove them?

Sometimes, as you can imagine, these conversations are tricky. Mostly, but not always, the parent in question will have removed themselves from a violent offender and/or be in some legal process to apply for an injunction, restraining order or non-molestation order against the perpetrator. Sometimes, there might be an understandable difficulty in distancing themselves from the perpetrator. When the next PPN comes in, you know that, in reality, they are still with said offender. That's when social care takes more of an interest. Sometimes we visit jointly with a social worker where there are concerns that a situation is escalating or has reached a dangerous level, or the child/children are witnessing violent offences.

These notifications are crucial to informing our work. If there is a child under five who is in a household such as this, the health visitor will assess the impact of the situation on that child. Is their development and/or behaviour being impacted? We can then offer the appropriate intervention: a parenting course or a 'Freedom' course, whereby one learns about changing patterns of behaviour, and how not to choose another violent/abusive partner. Sometimes if the services on offer are not being taken up or taken seriously, the mother (usually but not always) will have to make the choice between remaining in contact with the violent perpetrator or, ultimately, having the child or children removed.

In amongst these challenges, we contend with the latest trend of 'hot-desking'. We no longer have our own office, *per se*, or even our own specific desk or set of drawers – we are more likely to be in a 'hub' along with several other health visitors, community staff nurses, nursery nurses, admin ladies and the like. We will have a tray on a shelf with our mug and other bits and bobs in. It's invariably noisy, with phones trilling and constant chatter, and it can be hard to hear yourself think, especially if preparing a Child Protection Report.

But more often than not, the upsides outweigh the lack of personal space. There are a few male health visitors – I did work with one who was a student with me a few years ago – but overwhelmingly it is still a female profession. There is a shared sense of purpose, much jocularity and a real sisterhood.

We share our personal stories of family issues, relationship stuff and worries about children if we need to, and many of us do. There is support and mutual respect and love there. And lots of biscuits. If there is some perilous event to deal with, more often than not someone lovely will say, 'What can I do to help? Can I make you a drink?' It's a very sociable job and your colleagues contribute immensely to you feeling safe and ultimately to your wellbeing. They are pivotal, actually.

Sitting on sofas today, it is patently clear that most people wish to be listened to, respected, treated as a human being, rather than a process or an inconvenience. We are not algorithms. People yearn for the personal touch. A real person responding to another person with their histories, feelings, experiences, thoughts.

I do sometimes give some clients my own mobile number – usually the most vulnerable, because it guarantees they stay in touch. Somehow, knowing that they have a hotline to you reassures them that they can communicate when they need to, not just when we want them to. And interestingly, it's never abused. Not ever.

Recently, on a day off, one of my clients texted to say she was bleeding. On further questioning, it appeared she was having a post-partum haemorrhage – a severe bleed following the birth of her baby – and I had to call an ambulance; it was an emergency. I called her back to ensure she was still breathing and conscious; she had run out of sanitary towels and was cutting up nappies. Fortunately her partner was with her – he was organising childcare so he could accompany her to hospital. She was admitted and treated and went home, and I was able to follow her up.

Giving my personal mobile out to social workers ensures that they can liaise when they get a moment. I am occasionally on the blower to them in the evening at home, as that is the only time they have to share important information. It's a bit of a misconception to think that health visiting only happens from nine to five. We are often operating on our own time.

Tomorrow my day involves a visit to a girl who hasn't been seen by a health visitor for over a year. The child has not had any developmental assessment and is often reported to be grubby, speech-delayed and sullen when mum drops her off at nursery and departs quickly thereafter. I have tried on numerous occasions to access her, wondering what lies on the other side of the door. Whatever it is, we will help her to the very best of our abilities to enable her and her daughter to achieve the best life that they can lead, providing sustained support until they swim autonomously and unaided. I really hope to be able to help.

There is absolute joy in being able to help, to signpost or influence someone in the right direction, and by that I mean whatever is right for them.

Parenting is the hardest job we ever do, and when it's really tough it's good to be able to share your thoughts and feelings, and know where you can turn for advice. Just take something simple like colic, for instance – this is pretty much unfathomable, especially if you have tried everything available, from medicines such as Infacol or Colief to baby massage – or, if you're formula feeding, possibly a change of milk. We can offer our presence to discuss the feelings of inadequacy that so often arise when trying, unsuccessfully, to deal with issues such as this.

There are numerous other issues in the early weeks and months that need ironing out. Sleeplessness, exhaustion, altered family dynamics, relationship difficulties, lack of cash, bailiffs, housing problems, bereavement, employment issues, entitlement to and claiming of benefits, worries about baby's weight gain or lack of it. There are so many possible obstacles to encounter when you have had a baby. It's too easy, especially with the advent of social media like Instagram, to feel just a little bit inadequate or hopeless. We all feel those things at some point.

If you have family, then you may avail yourself of them, but there are many reasons why someone might not have ready access to a relative who can help. This is where health visitors provide an essential support service. They might just be the person to walk with you, to help you find your 'mojo', to make that 'down day' more bearable when they arrive on your doorstep, hopefully with a smile and a can-do attitude and, crucially, armed with a myriad of nursing, midwifery and health-visiting skills and experience.

We will try to enable you to come to your own conclusions and make sense of your particular situation, while offering a friendly 'You got this – you are so totally bossing it' – when you have convinced yourself that you really aren't at all. It can often be subtle. You might sometimes think, 'What did she do, exactly? She just sat on my sofa and drank tea, didn't she?' When, in reality, we might have discussed everything from breastfeeding to child development to maternity pay to colic to returning to work and what to look for when choosing a childminder. Hopefully, we enable you to make your own decisions – in the end, those are the very best kind.

There are few of us left who have coped with endless change and political interference with unfailing ingenuity, goodwill, resilience and lateral thinking. I should add that, as health care workers, our strapline is 'Excellence, Compassion and Expertise'. We strive to live up to that.

Despite the vagaries of expert opinion, risk assessment and a policy for virtually everything, sometimes we just don't know what we are going to be presented with. One of my colleagues visits a couple with a selection of toddlers and a couple of pythons. The latter get to watch TV on the sofa with the parents each evening when the kids have gone to bed. Another family keep a huge motorbike in the kitchen which also houses several large German shepherds. There is no room for anyone or anything else. You couldn't swing a chihuahua.

I have visited homes with bats in the attic (or belfry) which is always cause for much consternation; these creatures seemingly have more rights than you or I. One particular house had droppings dripping from the ceiling and, despite the health concerns of the children whose bedrooms were below (bats are terrible spreaders of disease), the bats, who are protected by domestic and international law, remained. It is unlawful to kill, take or injure a wild bat or disturb or obstruct access to a roost. The council could do very little about the situation. I wrote letter after letter and made endless calls. We badgered them until the family were rehoused, which took an age.

There is absolute joy and fulfilment in health visiting. Make no mistake, serving others is one of the best feelings ever – when you've written that housing letter and it made a difference (rare nowadays, but it can happen) or applied to that charity for a new washing machine for a family, because without one they cannot function – and it is not only granted, but delivered and plumbed in too. When someone smiles, looks perkier and sees themselves as a competent and loving mother, following many weeks when they very much didn't — but after a series of your visits, they turned it around.

Sometimes we have to acknowledge that you might not like us all of the time, but what other health professional gets to see you for such an extended period of time consistently and in your own home? Who else turns up and deals with your specific issues at your convenience and generally for an hour, or often more, with a promise to return as and when necessary and, again, at a time of your choosing?

Kindness has featured in lots of memoirs by health professionals recently, and for good reason. It is, I believe, a political act. It is an act of defiance in this miserable sodding world, where no one seems to care that you can't afford to get the food shop in this week due to unexpectedly steep bills and you feel like a crap mum as a consequence. Lots of us have been there. It might be a surprise to think that many health visitors have also experienced life with all its attendant issues. We don't get to sit on your sofa without knowing a thing or two.

I hope that the decision-makers in the NHS perceive the value in continuing to fund and develop the health visiting service. Without it, where will mothers go? And what will the social and emotional cost be if there is no one to turn to? Who will they approach when faced with what feels like an insurmountable problem when, in all likelihood, it might easily and readily be addressed by a wise and empathetic health visitor?

The GP hasn't got the time; often they can only deal with one single issue per appointment, directing us to make another one if we need to ask about something else (unless you get a marvellous GP who will happily chat about anything and everything – I have discovered some of those). Our wonderful nursery nurses deal brilliantly with specific issues such as sleep issues, potty training and behaviour management, but when it gets sticky and there are complex issues to be considered, the health visitor wins, hands down.

We have seen it all, mostly – drug dealing, prostitution, mental health issues, arguing on behalf of a client for resources, advocating for their housing, dropping off a food bank voucher, trying to stall the bailiffs, those battling with depression. Sometimes, only a health visitor will do. We are fearless champions of our clients, passionate about your wellbeing and always wanting the best for you. One of my mums commented this week: 'You're old school, you are – old school's best. I feckin' love you.' And, in that vein, we have loved you all, too. Every single one. Wanting the best for you and willing to help you achieve it if it's within our remit and capacity is the reason we turn up. If we can't help you, we will always find someone who can.

I am privileged to have worked and continue to work with health visitors who are wise and funny and have bags of integrity; some are single parents themselves and battle on alone and heroically, others care for elderly parents before and after work, some have health issues of their own, or maybe their partners or children do. Some are happy, some have faced total and utter disaster and still get up and at 'em, to visit the brave, beautiful, witty and wise multicultural British public, offering the very best that we have. We have been vulnerable too, you see. Sometimes, we still are.

So, now you know that, get the kettle on. Shall we sit? Sofa or floor? Yep, I'd love that coffee. Shall I hold baby so you can drink yours hot for a change? Tell me what you are worried about. Perhaps I can help.

I realise that you may well have been shocked along the way by some of my experiences. I make no apologies for this. When you peel back the layers in this glittery, easy-access communication age, all that is left is humanity in all of its guises. We feel the joy of being there, walking alongside you when something good happens in your life and helping when it isn't going quite so well.

So, why do we do it? What motivates us to get out of bed on a wet winter morning knowing full well what trials and ordeals lie ahead? The money? I think not. Anybody choosing to enter this profession for the money is likely to find themselves short-changed in very quick order. The truth is that it is a vocation, a calling if you will, not a job. My own view is that there is no greater calling than helping others. The act of giving even when life's events are pressing you hard demonstrates an enduring optimism.

You also get to meet absolutely everyone. You may find yourself sitting cross-legged on the floor with an Afghan family drinking black tea, an interpreter at your side; you might get to visit a family in a castle, a caravan or a converted bus, or a Polish family offering sweet treats; you might find yourself in a high-rise flat, a squat, a brothel, a homeless hostel, a politician's townhouse, a tattoo parlour – you just never know.

However, I think the following really nails it. It's attributed to Plato, although there are several others who lay claim to it, but it remains apt:

'Be kind, for everyone you meet is fighting a hard battle.'

It applies equally to the rich, professional woman, the refugee in a homeless hostel, the single mother in a squat and to the health visitor sitting in front of you.

Epilogue
Love in the Time of Corona

There is a deadly virus in our midst. Marauding around the globe, crowned with its glycan bonded spikes to disguise its viral proteins, which evade the immune system and violate the cells inside the surface of the lungs and airways. It is a 'wolf in sheep's clothing'. Unconscionable in its ambition, crushing its victims – yet surprisingly fragile, destroyed by an itty little bit of regular 20-second bouts of hand-washing. It is a perplexing beast, having taken hundreds of thousands of lives worldwide and over tens of thousands in the UK alone, at the time of writing.

We are in strange, safe distancing, muted and compliant Covid times. In the community, as NHS health visitors, we are offering telephone conversations and support, instead of our usual home visits. We are working not just from our office, but from home, often in our own time, on days off, during the evenings and at night, with parents who we have yet to meet in person. If there is a feeding concern, or a parent who is feeling overwhelmed and there are multiple worries, we can now visit – with gloves and aprons, masked up – in lockdown. Keys and pens in pockets and with minimal equipment carried in on the baby weighing scales. Cleaned before and after each use. That's the power of Azomax!

The NHS, as Boris Johnson says, is the 'beating heart of our nation'. It is also our respiratory system, puffing life into our most ailing and stricken via CPAP or mechanical ventilators. There's dissent about ventilator usage, of course. There's dissent about everything, from the hydroxychloroquine/Azithromycin/zinc combo to the rush for vaccines.

Will they appear this year?

What about testing?

Antigens – have I got it?

Antibodies – have I had it?

To mask or not? How, *exactly*, is it transmitted? Droplet infection? Tidal breath? Smear infection (the touching of surfaces and door handles)? Sneezing? Aerosolised faeces?

From where, exactly, does it originate? Lab? Bat? Pangolin?

Who is Neil Ferguson? And why is he running the country?

Does the NHS have capacity? Why didn't it initially?

Who took the minutes and outlined the action points for Operation Cygnus?

So many questions and all too few concrete answers.

Life, although somewhat attenuated and clearly more pedestrian for all of us in this time of lockdown, is ramping up for our PM, who mercifully recovered from his life-threatening infection. His expectant partner, Carrie Symonds, also exhibited symptoms. Both have expressed their sincere gratitude to the NHS and its talented staff.

Government aides appear to have been laid low and recovered, too. Chris Whitty, Chief Medical Officer – he of the kindly 'poached egg' eyes. Matt Hancock, Health Secretary, appears to have self-isolated. He also loves a badge bearing a four-letter word beginning with 'C'. No, not that one. Care! Then there's ex-nurse and health minister Nadine Dorries and, likely, many others.

There's been singing, clapping, the banging of pots, the lighting of candles, rainbows in windows and all forms of appreciation expressed in myriad ways. I have received gifts from fellow villagers – wine, flowers, even local venison. The chippy near the health centre in Littlemoor, Weymouth offered all local NHS staff free sausage and chips. Various cafes gave away free coffees. Thank you so very much.

We will have called neighbours to see if we can help, in some way, shopping or similar. We will have Facetimed friends and relatives, Zoomed or Web-Ex'd colleagues; case conferences for us health visitors have taken place via Skype or conference calls. I.T. has calamitously let us down on a few occasions, but come up roses for the most part. The NHS has developed an app contact tracing those who may test positive for Covid-19.

There are 750,000 NHS Volunteers who wish to play their part in this nationwide mission, all of whom are heroes. Along with postmen and women, refuse/recycling collectors, supermarket staff and food bank volunteers (whose valuable work will be even more in demand now, with the downturn in the economy).

There were a million requests for Universal Credit in the first few weeks of this lockdown. Some people have been furloughed, some are on reduced hours and many, very sadly, will have lost their jobs. Some, still in employment, will have purchased extra items to place in the food bank trolley at their supermarket. Some will have set up a standing order to their nearest food bank to ensure a regular flow of income for them.

Shocking statistics for domestic abuse have been reported as charities write to the government to ask for more assistance. Hotels have been approached to open up rooms for those fleeing violence.

Yet, in amongst all this uncertainty and worse, there are extraordinary events unfolding. Possibly, the rethinking of small things, like shopping. Maybe, you're tired of queueing

Soviet style for the supermarket, only to be harangued over the tannoy suggesting you 'complete your shopping as quickly as possible'. After 45 minutes of waiting to get in, I hadn't thought of that...

But maybe, as a result, you've discovered a farm shop that delivers locally grown produce, or the village butcher who cycles your sausages and slices of smoked streaky to the door. Or you have woken up to the early morning joy that is the milk delivery to your doorstep.

Is it me, or do the birds sound chirpier? Fluffing, flitting and frolicking, arguing noisily, in and out of the privet using a very clever 'one-way' system. And the bees! *So* many, spotted hovering lazily in the borders of my scruffy garden. (Ground elder a speciality). Speaking of gardens, whose grinchy and sclerotic heart cannot fail to be captivated by Captain Tom Moore? Just turned 100 and gamely walking laps of his garden aided by his trusty frame to raise millions for the NHS. What a guy! Made of marvellous and magnificent stuff. Go Tom!

Various UK companies have vowed to manufacture PPE for NHS staff. Distilleries including Black Cow vodka and breweries such as Brew Dog have reconfigured their output to include alcohol hand sanitisers. Gin distilleries are getting in on the act, too. The contents of the hand gel have to be denatured, of course, to prevent people drinking them!

In all of this outpouring of kindness, generosity and ingenuity, there are some puzzling aspects to human behaviour which I won't even try to understand. Fighting in the supermarket aisles over loo roll! Those who spit and cough at frontline workers – 'here, have some corona'. Those who leave snippy notes on cars when they have no clue as to who is a key worker and who isn't. For all those jawless bottom-feeders there are no words. Their idea of a moral compass is navigating and disseminating hatred of all that is good, *and they will not win*. Kindness always wins in the end.

The NHS was founded on kindness, on doing the right thing. Its guiding principle is that it is funded through general taxation and free at the point of delivery. It is worthwhile noting that before its creation, on 5 July 1948, individuals and families were pushed into debt in order to pay for a medical consultation. Doctors were threatening to boycott this new NHS as late as February 1948.

My own grandfather pursued medical treatment for an infected leg ulcer, knowing his condition was preventing him from working, leaving him unable to support his family. He felt compelled to try and get it treated so, in the 1930s, he left nine children in the workhouse to travel to London in an attempt to get it fixed. Treatments were costly and variable in their efficacy. But free healthcare was on its way. The NHS brought together nurses, pharmacists, doctors, opticians, dentists and hospitals for the first time in this giant UK-wide organisation. It was and remains a visionary service. It has its faults and at some point, there will possibly be an analysis: what did the NHS do well in these covid times? And what did it do less well?

There will be a time of evaluation and possibly reform, but we cannot throw the baby out with the bath water.

The NHS is our national crown, our seal of civilisation and beacon of moral leadership. During its lifetime, the NHS has seen and facilitated numerous significant break-throughs, directly impacting and improving our wellbeing – from diphtheria and polio vaccines in the 1940s/50s to pneumococcal meningitis in 2006 and all of the vaccines in between. Our immunisation programme is a cornerstone of the nation's wellbeing.

There was the discovery of the link between smoking and cancer, and the attendant ban on smoking in public places in 2006, the discovery of DNA, the contraceptive pill, available only to married women in the early 60s and made more widely available in 1967. The Abortion Act – again in 1967 – before which women were forced to seek back street terminations, many dying of sepsis as a result. There have been heart and kidney transplants, CT scans, test-tube babies, and so forth.

We have all benefitted from the NHS regardless of our political persuasion, and it's easy to take its presence and accessibility for granted, like a hovering and devoted spouse, only to realise after their demise that you needed and relied on them after all. Imagine that appointment with the GP that you kept making and repeatedly missed because you were busy at work and the boss wouldn't let you leave? It might cost you financially in the future. That arthritis in your hip might impact you financially and physically if you don't have the insurance for the replacement. And in retirement, with limited resources, you might not be able to pay for it outright. That newly acquired diagnosis of type one diabetes might bring numerous and ongoing treatments – and what happens if you lose your job and any accompanying package of healthcare insurance? There is a myriad of reasons to be concerned about losing our crowning glory, our NHS. It's too easy to think that because it's always been there, it always will be.

I don't think for one moment that there is an appetite to change it out of all shape and recognition. I'm guessing that many will say it's 'top-heavy' in terms of managers. They may well be right. But I feel that this national crisis may clear the pathway for the right changes. Abandoning hospital car parking charges completely, improvements in terms of service delivery with reduced waiting times for operations and in

A&E, more GP appointments, pay-rises for nurses and their student debt cancelled, too?

Maybe this weird hiatus will bring some lateral and meaningful thinking. There will be many policy-makers who can focus on all of these things but for now, we should celebrate our many NHS heroes in all guises, the frontline nurses, doctors and care home staff who selflessly continue and devote themselves to their patients long after their contracted hours, hungry, barely able to function, whilst comforting the dying and the bereaved. In wholly inadequate PPE, on low pay, they put themselves at risk on every shift, leading to their own unjust demise in some instances.

We must continue to bang the drum for the NHS.

Consider how life would be without it. Here we are in the middle of a Covid-19 pandemic. There are no discriminators; it hospitalised our own PM, it has taken many lives, rich and poor, professional or otherwise, young and old. The scientists are working on a vaccine to be offered, but at some point there will be something else that challenges us globally, as a community or individually. That's the thing with illness and disease; it strikes unexpectedly and inconveniently.

Now, imagine that you've lost your job as many have, or you've lost a loved one, or you're elderly in receipt of a state pension with little savings. Then suppose you have to pay, either in cash, or via insurance (where someone else decides if you're covered or not) for that urgent hospital admission and the expert nursing care received, and the operation that the expensive doctor said you needed, and the anaesthetist's time, and the X-rays applied and scans undertaken and blood tests ordered and chemo and transfusions administered and the intravenous meds – and then envisage, for one dire moment, that you couldn't afford to pay for *any* of it.

Now tell me that our collective, idealistic, starry-eyed, uniquely British obsession with our beloved NHS is not warranted.

Acknowledgements

Grateful and humble thanks to Jo Sollis, Executive Editor of Mirror Books who has generously championed me and for her humour, warmth and serenity. I somehow felt that you knew what I was thinking before I did! Thank you so much to Rebecca Winfield, of David Luxton Associates, my brilliant, funny, and wise Literary Agent for cheerleading me and for your touching belief in, not just my story, but in health visiting, particularly. Huge thanks to Liz Marvin, my Editor, whose extraordinary wizardry is a spectacle to behold – thank you for your clarity and for your hard work. Many thanks to Melanie Sambells and Sarah Harwood in Publicity for their enthusiasm and diligence and to the whole marketing and publicity team.

Thank you, Jenny Smith, Specialist Midwife, Lecturer, Founder of The Jentle Midwifery Scheme and Author for an all-too-brief but important exchange and for reminding me of your enduring, calm wisdom.

Acknowledgements

Special mention to Pat Gallagher of Writing Buddies, the splendid writing group at Dorchester Library where I first found my 'voice' and the confidence to submit my work to Literary Agents.

And, of course, Jan Thorp, tireless and indefatigable Health Visitor and Field Work Teacher. Thank you for your expert tutelage and support all those years ago.

Thank you to my colleagues, past and present, of all disciplines, in Devon, London and Dorset but especially to my fantastic colleagues at Littlemoor Health Centre, Weymouth – Michelle, Jade, Jane, Ali, Tracey, Lisa H. Carol, Debbie, Janet, Teresa, Jakki, Emma B, Emma T, Katie P, Katie H, Myra, Lorna, Belinda, Julie, Natalie, Lisa W, Brie, Alex, Louise, Jodie – get the bourbons in! Sara, Gill, Mary, Denise, Rachel, Mel, Sharon, Jules, Jan, Amy, Leanne, Juliet – honorary HV, you are the bestest Milk Monitor, ever. Kay & Bev – miss you loads and love you all!

Author Biography

Rachael has worked in the NHS for 40 years as a Nurse and Midwife, having trained at Bart's and St Thomas' & Guy's respectively. For the last 30 years she has worked as a Health Visitor, having plied her trade in Devon, Hackney, Tower Hamlets and Dorset. She has been a Practice Teacher, and in her thirties, thought it would be a good idea to do a Master's when she was working full-time, had a five-year-old and was expecting her second child. Rachael dipped a toe into line management some years ago but decided it wasn't for her, much preferring the front line of Health Visiting, where she remains to date.

Rachael is married to J. and they live in Dorset. They love Cornwall, Border Collies and perfecting home-made Damson Gin. They have two grown-up children whom they adore.